W9-ATZ-985

The Yoga of Golf

Copryight © 2003 Ronald L. Mann
All rights reserved. No part of this book may be reproduced or
transmitted in any form or by any means, electronic or mechanical,
including photcorpying, recording, or by any information stroage and
retrieval system, without written permission of the publisher.

Published by
IAH
16070 W. Sunset Blvd., #306
Pacific Palisades, CA 90272
866-816-1026

ISBN: 0-9710605-4-1, $29.95 paper

First Edition

Cover Designed by Mike Andolina
Yoga Postures by Suzanne Strachan
Photographs by Dan Steinberg

Library of Congress Cataloging-in-Publication Data

Printed in the United States of America

TESTIMONIALS

"One of the most daunting tasks for a golf instructor is to teach the student to stay in the present. Amateur golfers constantly berate themselves for a poor last shot or mentally project what they believe they will score for the day. Dr. Mann supplies excellent techniques to help the golfer with both concentration and the ability to live in the present.

The Yoga of Golf is readable, well structured and informative for both the professional and the striving, amateur golfer. I urge all my students to read and practice the techniques clearly taught in The Yoga of Golf."

Patrick Boyd, Golf Professional at MoutainGate CC.

Pat is a former Hogan (Nike) Tour player and is best remembered for the year he won the Utah Open, the Northern California Open and the Alaska Open all with course records. A holder of 11 course records nationally, Boyd is still the course record holder at these California courses: Adobe Creek in Petaluma; Bayonet Course at Fort Ord; Boundary Oak in Walnut Creek; Chardonnay Vineyards in Napa; Club Shakespeare; Napa; Fountain Grove in Santa Rosa; and Sonoma National in Sonoma California.

"Dr. Mann was a huge part of our success, and has been a great educator for the team and for me as a coach. I am thrilled to report that with Dr. Mann's help, our team, which had not qualified for the National Championship since 1977, not only qualified, but also finished in 5th place. I would recommend him to any golfer that wants to explore some of the deeper mental aspects of golf in hopes to lower their score. "

Carrie Leary
Head Coach
UCLA Women's Golf

TABLE OF CONTENTS

ACKNOWLEDGMENTS

I want to thank Suzanne Strachan for her expertise and talent regarding the asana section. Her contributions and insight resulted in greater clarity and precision for this section. She also served as the model for all postures.

There are also several people who have been instrumental in the development and support of this book either through direct or indirect support. I am deeply greateful to: Merry Aronson, Lee Brandon, Patrick Boyd, Jeff Jackson, Bob Fisher, Mei Ling Moore, and Larry Payne.

FOREWORD

by Lee Brandon, C.S.C.S.
(Certified Strength and Conditioning Specialist, 2001 RE/MAX World Long Drive Champion)

WARNING!

IF you are NOT open to changing your life and ultimately your game,
DO NOT read this book!

Dr. Ron Mann's enlightened research and views have provided me with the tools and techniques that have guided me in a direction of self- exploration and self-management; resulting in greater performance in the extreme pressure of competition. *The Yoga of Golf* is not narrowly defined by what most people think of as Yoga, i.e. the physical stretching postures. Dr. Mann provides a much broader perspective that skillfully integrates the "union" of mind, body, emotions, and spirit.

Being a Conditioning Specialist, I know that a specific stretching protocol might not fit for everyone. Because we are all so different, each individual needs to consider her/his body, strength and flexibility. However, Dr. Mann provides a foundation and map for mental and spiritual flexibility that is universally applicable to all who want to enhance their sport's performance.

Golf is a pressure cooker that magnifies all weaknesses. It has forced me to evaluate all aspects of my life. I have personally worked with Dr. Mann and have benefited from his sensitivity, wisdom and insights. He has skillfully shared his knowledge and approach in *The Yoga of Golf.* I feel this book provides valuable guidelines and the road map for anyone seriously interested in peak performance. This information will help you take all aspects of your game and life to another level.

Dr. Mann's approach forced me to take an honest look at every aspect of my life and game! He does not teach something he does not live! His life and "way of being" provides a down to earth example and makes him ultimately credible to me. He has challenged me to deeply explore the internal factors that effect success on every level and I have seen the fruits of that work. If you are committed to taking your life and game to the next level, read this book!

PREFACE

The Yoga of Golf represents what I have learned from thirty years of yoga and meditation practice and over forty years of playing sports. I was eight years old when I began playing baseball in the Little League. It turns out I had a talent. I was a left-handed pitcher with a knuckle ball. I could switch hit being somewhat ambidextrous. Our team was good and we went to the Little League World Series sponsored by the Western Boys Baseball Association. We placed second. During Middle School I played in Pony League. I hold the league pitching record of 14 wins and no loses. I hit .491.

These were magical times for me. I had more fun playing baseball than anything else in my life. I remember being at bat and a rectangle appeared right before the pitcher. As soon as he released the ball I knew if it would be in the strike zone or not. If the ball was in the rectangle it was a good pitch. I was able to pick up the ball in less than a second after it left his hand.

During High School I was offended by the baseball coache's style, since he primarily worked as the football coach. He was out for blood and that was not my experience of baseball. He treated us like football players. I left the baseball team and moved over to the golf team. I was fortunate to be at Santa Monica High School in Southern California. Riviera Country Club was our home course, and I was able to play Riviera twice a week. For the rest of my life, golf became my game of choice.

During my youth I would play golf and have moments of such joy. I was having so much fun I could not contain my laughter. I was in beautiful surroundings, in harmony with nature and sinking chip shots off the green for birdies. There was no effort; the more joy I felt, the better I played. As adults it is usually the other way around. If we play well, then we are happy.

As a young adult in my late twenties, I began to practice hatha yoga and meditation. After receiving my Ph.D., I began to work with terminally ill children. Death can be a great teacher. I was blessed to have many spiritual experiences that helped me with those difficult patients and their parents. I was given a deeper understanding regarding our true nature and the eternity of the soul. I was shown how the mind limits us from greater wisdom and greater expression.

My study of yoga and my professional work changed my relationship to everyday life. I moved to a different context and paradigm regarding life's purpose. I was no longer primarily concerned about outcomes and performance, but more interested in quality, learning, love, growth and development. I knew that we were given opportunities to learn from everything we did, and the learning was as, if not more, important as the final outcomes.

Yoga and meditation opened up a new inner dimension of subtle energies that Western psychology did not understand or explain. Studies in consciousness spoke to these realities and I found that I could actually manifest more positive results in every aspect of my life, i.e. work, love and sports, if I embraced the inner reality in all that I did. On many occasions I would play nine holes of golf after a weekend meditation retreat. I would spend four to six hours a day in deep meditative states and move beyond the limited perception of myself as body, mind or emotions. During those few days I would not think about golf and would not touch a golf club. The next day, I would go out late in the afternoon, still feeling the peace and reverie from the deep mediation, and shoot scratch or one over. I was impressed how little effort it took and how open and free I felt.

There is an interesting Native American story about a tribe that was suffering a great drought. Out of desperation they finally contacted the "rainmaker" to help them.

The rainmaker arrived at the village on a very, very dry day. Upon arrival he asked for his tent. He went inside and did not come out. After the first day the tribesmen were worried. What is he doing in there and when is he going to help us.

Upon the second day, clouds began to appear in the horizon. The rainmaker still remained in his tent. With day three, more dark clouds began to roll in and by the end of the day it was pouring rain. The tribesmen were overjoyed.

The rainmaker finally emerged from his tent and the tribe asked him how he accomplished this great feat. He explained, "It is actually very simple. When I arrived I could feel that things were not in order here. Some things were not in harmony. So, I went to my tent to bring myself in harmony with all that IS. I know that if I am in harmony, then all will unfold around me in the proper order of things. There had been a long drought and it was not in the proper order of things. I knew if I was in harmony, then all would be well. It is in the proper order of nature to rain, thus the rain came!"

The Yoga of Golf is about finding the proper order or harmony within us, so we can play our best. It is the nature order of life to express ourselves in the best way we can. Typically, we get in our own way. If we are in harmony with ourselves, then we get out of the way and let our best emerge and express itself.

Yoga actually means "union". Within this spiritual context union typically refers to the Divine, however, union with nature and all of creation brings us to deeper aspects of ourselves. It is said that we are made in the image and likeness of God. So, our perfection is encoded within us. The Yoga of Golf provides the map for finding our way home.

The entire scope of yoga is vast and thousands of books have been written about is varies aspects. This book is not a definitive statement about yoga. It does provide the essence of yoga practice and clearly demonstrates how these approaches will improve your golf game. If you want to learn more about yoga as a system, the reader is encouraged to continue his/her study in that direction.

The Yoga of Golf will help your golf game and transform your life. I hope you will enjoy it.

Ron Mann, Ph.D.

INTRODUCTION

The Yoga of Golf
How to stop your mind and still stay awake!

One mind cannot be put to two uses.
Chinese proverb

Equipment is the key to success? The best way to lower your score is to buy a new driver. Right or Wrong? Probably wrong. This is the conventional wisdom that is presented in 99% of all ads for golf. Get the "Killer Bee" driver and take four strokes off your game. Buy the "whatever" putter and shave three strokes off your game. The club manufacturers would like us to believe that golf is mostly a mechanical game, and better balls, gloves and clubs will make us better players.

I do believe equipment is important. Well-fitted clubs will make a difference to the better player. However, equipment is not the answer to a consistently lower score.

The Yoga of Golf is about the deeper truth regarding peak performance. You can learn to play in the Zone if you attend to your inner-life, along with your mechanics.

Mechanics are the key? TV announcers would have us believe that swing mechanics is what really accounts for great golf shots. What do you typically see on TV after a mishit? The announcer quickly provides an instant recap with the telestrator and a quick review with the lines and arrows showing where the swing came off plane. While these mechanics details are true, the question is seldom, if ever, asked, "What prompted the player to mishit the ball?"

Most PGA tour players have exceptional mechanical skill and the best equipment money can buy. It is really a question of the chicken and the egg. What came first? Did the player have some unseen, internal mental/emotional reaction that caused him or her to lose tempo or concentration, or was it simply a physical breakdown that led to the mishit?

Just for the record, I believe that mechanics are important. If you do not have some basics covered, it is very difficult, if not impossible to score well. A strong mental game does not replace very poor mechanics. However, mechanics alone are not the answer!

The mind? In physical medicine it has been established that about 80% of all visits to a physician are stress related. Thus, what starts in the mind and goes through the emotions ultimately ends up in the physical body. Stress begins in the mind and most problems in competitive play are the result of stress related issues that originate in the mind.

We never hear an announcer wonder what was going through a player's mind just before he or she hit a shot. Perhaps that would be too much of a personal intrusion on national TV. However, the truth of the matter is that the internal thoughts and subconscious feelings are more likely to affect a player's success on a given day than their equipment or swing mechanics.

Annika Sörenstam, the number one ranked woman golfer on the LPGA Tour, was recently asked on 60 Minutes, "What is the strongest part of your game?" She replied, "My mental game!"

To the credit of the golf world, a recognition of stress and mental pressure is beginning to appear on national TV during PGA events. Jim Nantz, Lanny Wadkins, and Peter Kostas of CBS Sports discussed Annika's poorer performance on day two of the Bank of America Colonial. The first day was very stressful for here with all the media attention and controversy regarding her participation. She shot at 71 on the first day, one over par, and had a chance to make the cut. Day two was different. She ended up +5 and the cut was plus 1. She missed the cut by four strokes. During the round, the commentators observed that she looked mentally worn out from all the stress of the previous day. They related her different mental condition to her swing. It was a well integrated discussion regarding body and mind.

Success: Woody Allen said "Eighty percent of success is showing up." Success on or off the course is directly related to some basic psychological factors; determination, positive self-esteem and freedom from self-destructive internal dialogue are three important ones. One must be at peace and feel good about oneself to succeed in life, no matter what your work is. Perseverance is everything. You can never give up. Vince Lombardi said, "If you can't accept losing, you can't win."

Breakdown, therefore, certainly has some specific psychological or mental components, but what about success? We know more about what keeps people for succeeding than we do about unbelievable, out of the box, success. Tiger Woods is a good example. His great accomplishments, I suggest, are the result of more than just good mechanics, excellent conditioning, and sound mental game. His Buddhist influence and meditative training help to create a field of consciousness, an energy that directly affects physical, material reality. Most sports psychology books talk about the mind from a psychological perspective and leave it at that.

Managing breakdown and the ability to recover is the key to ultimate success on the course. There are no perfect rounds. The player's ability to bounce back from a bad shot and recover from bad lies, bad bounces and bad swings is the key to success.

Beyond the mind: *The Yoga of Golf* takes us to the next level: consciousness is beyond the mind, beyond thought. It

4

is the terrain of breakthrough performance. It is the state where object and observer unite. It is the oneness that we all strive for in so many unconscious ways.

Balance, personal mastery, realization of one's highest potential, integrity, honesty, and the evolution of the self: are we referring to golf or yoga? Golf is an interesting game because it is actually non-competitive and played against oneself. The golf swing is very, very sensitive to what is in the mind. The more you think, the poorer you play! The golfer excels when personal mastery over inner demons of fear, doubt, negativity and unwanted mental chatter are achieved.

Golf has gained greater interest in the last few years because of Tiger Woods' dynamic success. It is not widely known that his mother is a Buddhist and he was brought up in a meditative environment that has taught him skills, techniques and a philosophy for personal mastery. His mother's influence was an important balance to the rigorous training Tiger received from his father, a military man who helped Tiger develop strength, toughness and the warrior instinct. This balance between the masculine and feminine is what makes Tiger great.

Yoga: The system of yoga, widely misunderstood to focus only upon the body, is actually designed to help achieve realization of the self or soul. The word "yoga" actually means

5

union. The goal is to achieve a state of non-duality where there is no separation between the self and the universe. The cosmic forces of love and wisdom are expressed by one's very Being. The individual, personal identity becomes one with the greater forces of Life. Actions, thinking and doing give rise to a different way of being that allows for a more authentic expression of the self. Joy is the result.

Help from above: Jim, age 46, called me a few years ago. He told me the following story.

"My father was a scratch golfer (zero handicap) and wanted me to play golf. I never really wanted to do so and always rebelled. He died when I was a teenager and I took up the game as a way to honor him. I guess I had it in my genes because I was a good golfer. I could shoot 68 without much problem. I was in a tournament as a young man and was not doing too well. At one point I looked up to heaven and said to my Dad, "I thought you had more pull up there." I felt this tingling sensation in my spine and a lighter feeling in my body. I went on the birdie the next seven holes in a row. My only regret was that I ran out of holes to play!"

Jim wanted to know if I could help him find this state again.

Those familiar with yoga practice know that tingling sensation to be the subtle life force energy or kundalini moving up the spine. The lightness of being is common to a shift into higher states of awareness. Prayer and devotion often trigger some sort of "divine response" to help us in times of need. Perhaps it is possible to consciously tap into something greater than ourselves.

In the recent past the captain of the United States Rider Cup team, Ben Crenshaw, told his team he had a "feeling" that they would do well. Mr. Crenshaw was a very devout man and his feeling was some sort of divine intuitive knowing. The team did come back from behind to win.

Zone: Those who have ever touched the Zone know the joy that exists when effort ceases and each swing has a rhythm and timing that results in great shots and long putts falling dead center in the hole. I believe we can learn something from the yoga system and consciously apply it to golf to increase our chances to find the magic and wonder that keeps us coming back to play this difficult and challenging game.

Yoga is perfect for golf because that system provides the philosophy and techniques to bring an individual into a state of inner harmony, balance and awareness that allows for the inherent capacities and abilities to emerge. We know the Zone is a special place without a sense of time, without a sense of separation of self from object (ie., the hole seems bigger, closer; the greens seem more reachable, the greens are easier to read and feel), and an ability to perform without effort.

The Zone, as we know it, is a familiar place for those who practice yoga: peace of mind, a sense of connection, grace, joy, and effortlessness is that ultimate goal of yoga practice. The physical yoga techniques of stretching called *asana* and the mental training of meditation provide the student with the technology to move past the limitations of the mind and emotions. Peak performance in golf results when the golfer is able to effectively manage one's inner life, not be distracted by negative thoughts of doubt and fear, not be seduced into focusing on score and outcome, but rather stay in the moment and be with the unfolding process. Furthermore, the successful golfer must maintain trust in himself/herself even after a bad swing.

Beyond the ego: It has been said there is only "love or fear:" The love of the game, the love of self or the fear of failure, the fear of defeat or the fear of humiliation. Golf is yoga in action. Great golf offers us the opportunity to rise above the ego that is self-absorbed, self-consumed and always "trying" to accomplish something. The sage advice from the Bhagavad Gita "action without action, " and "not being identified with the fruits of the labor" lead one to play this game from a different perspective.

Golf is a paradoxical game because less is more. Trying

hard and swinging out of your shoes results in tremendous frustration and terrible results. Playing within your limits and being in harmony with nature, i.e. the golf course, leads to smart decisions and great rewards.

Most golfers have not realized that there is a deeper part of the self that knows how to hit a ball. This inner self has good timing, good tempo and a sense of how to roll the ball to make a good putt. This inner self actually has a lot more fun playing because it is a state where effort and doing are not the primary tasks at hand. A sense of being, an ability to trust and an ability to "Be" is available from this deeper self.

Contrast the above experience of Being, balance, harmony, and acceptance with the typical scene on the golf course. The golfer shows up with lots of apprehension, especially if money is on the line. One's ego is foremost since the first tee usually has some spectators and no one wants to look bad in front of others. The mind is filled with doubt about one's capacity to hit the first Tee-shot well. There is usually a lot of physical tension that results from the mental stress and expectations that have been created. With luck, the average golfer will at least hit the ball in the fairway and be off the first tee. The worst is that the first ball goes in the woods or the fairway bunker. It is not uncommon for men to just accept all this as fate and just take a mulligan and hope the next shot will find the fairway.

So the typical golf experience has the golfer arrive late, rush out of the car to the first tee without any physical warm-up, filled with dread and high expectations, or low expectations with a wishful fantasy to play at a level that is totally unrealistic, mishit their first shot, go into reaction with more fear, frustration and anger, drive off onto the fairway in search of their ball with the cursing of "Jesus..., God..... What an idiot..... " still floating in the subtle ether on the first tee. Thus we have begun a wonderful day in nature. Is this anyway to play this game? There is a better way!

Who is the competition? Golf like yoga is non-competitive in the sense that you are ultimately playing against yourself. Your biggest opponent is your ego, your self-doubt, your fear, your lack of faith and trust. Your biggest ally is your faith, your trust and your ability to accept what life brings to you. Thus, the deeper union with your essential self does allow you to play this game from an entirely different frame of reference.

The techniques and attitudes of yoga: breath, awareness, surrender, presence, acceptance, non-attachment, warrior like perseverance, and discipline lead to extraordinary performance. Not only does one's golf game improve, but one's character becomes refined and the rewards found on the links tend to impact family and work as well. The principles and techniques found here relate to all aspects of life, love, family and work.

Asthanga Yoga: The entire yoga system is known as Asthanga Yoga, Raja Yoga or the Eight Fold Path. It actually includes the following steps.

Yama and Niyama: Right behavior and action.
Asana: Physical postures.
Pranayama: Life force energy control through the breath.
Pratyahara: Internalization of the mind and the senses.
Dharana: Concentration.
Dhyana: Contemplation.
Samadhi: Oneness with creation.

All of these steps directly apply to golf and will help the golfer to find greater skill and joy in their game if appropriately applied.

I hope you enjoy the material presented. I know it can improve your life, on and off the course.

CHAPTER 1

Who is Hitting the Ball?

In the attitude of silence the soul finds the path in a clearer light, and what is elusive and deceptive resolves itself into crystal clearness
—Mahatma Gandhi

Ramana Maharshi is regarded as one of the greatest spiritual teachers that India has ever produced. He taught that one should engage in the self-inquiry "Who Am I?"

"Am I this hand?" "No"

"Am I this feeling?" No, it passes and I still remain."

"Am I this desire?"

"Am I job?"

The result of such relentless inquiry brings the realization that the true Self is eternal and beyond the limited definition of mind, body, position, material acquisition or emotion.

"Who Am I?" is not just an abstract esoteric question. It is actually a very down-to-earth, practical matter regarding who is hitting the ball.

Our understandings of personality development and consciousness have much to contribute here. Johnny Miller has told a story that is very relevant. During a Master's Tournament, which he ultimately won, he was on the last green. He needed to sink a thirty-foot putt to win. He felt his heart in his throat and was so nervous that he thought he could not make the putt. He did a very fascinating thing. He thought about his son and knew that his son could make the shot. He made a very clever shift in his mind and became his son. He knew his son could sink the putt. He imagined that his son was stroking the ball, and it dropped dead center. He won!

Ego states: Who is playing golf? This actually changes throughout the round, however, most people are not aware of the subtle changes in their internal personality that account for changes in their game. Which aspect of your personality is confident, secure and committed? Which part of your inner self is filled with doubt, fear, and apprehension? These various parts of the self have been referred to as "ego states." These are the different aspects of you that have been learned through social conditioning. They are like different roles you play in life. When you are at work, for example, you often have a different personality than when you are in your role as husband, wife, mother, father, son, daughter, etc.

13

Your performance varies when you shift states. Have you noticed how your performance decreases when you are attempting to prove something on the course? You want to show how far you can hit the ball and it is not your best shot. You actually get in your own way and limit your best performance when you are trying to do something.

Paradox: This is the paradox of golf. The less you do, the greater you play. The "you" in this case refers to your "ego." The part of you that is "trying" as opposed to the deeper part of yourself that "allows" something to happen. Too much effort, too much thinking, too much "trying" to perform are all functions of your ego getting in the way. Hence, the less you do, the less your ego is trying to do, the better you will play. Your game will come from a deeper, more trusting place within you.

The physical reality of a golf swing is based upon club speed, which is generated by coiling up like a spring and then unwinding. As your body unwinds, your arms follow. If you have an optimal state of tension, not too tense and not too relaxed, you will create the greatest club head speed. This is not accomplished through gross muscle movement. The ego, or that part of you that wants to hit the ball a mile, is by nature trying to accomplish something from the mind. Effort in golf actually creates tension and constriction, hence, less flexibility and fluidity and loss of distance. Furthermore, effort, trying and maintaining a focus upon results actually creates a separation between you and the desired goal, i.e., the target.

Separation and unity: Separation exists because the ego lives in a state of separation. The deeper self is unified and in harmony with life and nature. There is an interesting story from the Buddhist tradition. A student is sitting with his master and asks, "Master, how is it that you always know what I am thinking?" The Master replies, "My son, it is very simple. When we are together I hearing someone thinking and I know it is not me." Individuals who have a gift for healing also know this state. In the inner stillness and connection to the deeper self, they can perceive what is happening in another. It is through this intuitive perception or knowing that they are able to diagnose physical and emotional imbalances.

Quantum physics has revealed that we live in a sea of inter-connecting fields of energy. Consciousness is actually measurable vibrational patterns or forces. Our thought generates these fields and our mere existence is a state of consciousness. Everything in nature is a vibration with these subtle fields. While, individual awareness of these subtle energetic realms may vary, their existence and impact is continual.

Something special and magical happens when we find ourselves in harmony with the universe. We might hear a pro say, "The cup just kept getting in the way of the ball." "Everything just fell in." "I felt great and everything went my way." Getting out of our own way is the key. Bagger Vance advises us to "open to the field."

The sage advice to play each shot, one at a time, and be in the moment can only happen when you let go of your ideas regarding "what should be happening" and "how you want the round to unfold." Thus, having no expectations can lead to the greatest success. The only way to release all expectations is to get beyond the ideas of how you should play. The mind has lots of ideas about how things should go. "I want to get par." "I want to hit fairways and greens." What ultimately matters is that the ball goes into the hole. How you get there does not appear on the scorecard. The deeper self does not have preconceived ideas. It merely IS. Golf provides a fascinating challenge to learn how to bring this deeper self to the game.

The essential self: Studies in consciousness have explored deeper aspects of our nature and reveal another realm of internal differentiation. Most people believe that they are defined by what they think and feel. As far back as Descartes, "I think therefore I am," we have believed that our identities and existence are defined by our capacity to think. We also tend to give great weight to our emotional lives. We often define ourselves based upon our emotional states.

New perspectives have emerged in the West over the last decade regarding the nature of one's being, however, these truths have been known for thousands of years in the East. Individuals have observed that a deeper sense of identity or foundation of being exists that is different from thought or emotion. This aspect of one's inner nature has been called by various names: the essential self, the authentic self, the higher self, or the soul. This inner self resides at the core of our being. People typically discover this aspect of themselves through contemplative methods like meditation or deep prayer.

Nature of the Self

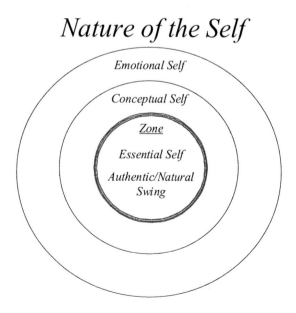

However, athletes have also discovered this inner terrain. This deeper inner self is free from the transitory thoughts of the mind or the changing moods of the emotions. This essential self is centered in a realm of peace, joy and wisdom. This deeper self is free from the limiting definitions of the mind that often tell us we cannot do this or that because it "just simply cannot

Nature of the Self

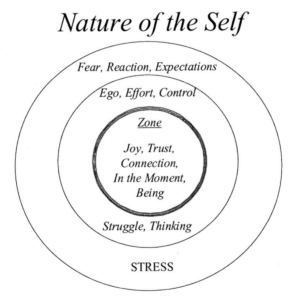

be done." The four-minute mile example directly speaks to the power of the mind.

Our consciousness is like the layers of an onion. Outer layers or membranes surround our inner self. The essential self is encapsulated by the body consciousness, the mind and the emotions. Inner clarity and freedom for peak expression and performance result when one realizes the inner, essential self and can distinguish between the deeper inner self and the outer manifestation of the body, mind and emotions. One achieves this inner clarity by learning to quiet the mind, withdraw the focus of attention away from the outer sensory world, and peacefully sit in the radiance of the soul. Freedom to live life to its fullest, and play golf at our best, results when we realize the true nature of consciousness and experience the deeper, essential self, untouched by the limiting ideas of the linear, rational mind.

The deeper essential self does not have preconceived ideas or attachments to outcome. It is not weighted down by worries or fears. It merely exists at the center of your being. In essence, it is the deeper expression of who you really are.

The Zone is this place of essential being and peak performance. Our inner connection yields great results without effort and with much more joy. The effort needed is learning how to access this internal state of balance and harmony in the midst of outer activity and a round of golf. It actually takes a lot of work and practice to learn how to stay connected to the deeper self. The work is about letting go and learning to detach from the mental and emotional factors that impair your ability to play your best.

Summary: In summary, the emotional factors that interfere with our essential connection to self are fear, emotional reactivity to bad shots (anger, frustration, contraction) and expectations that keep us out of the moment.

The mental factors that undermine our peak performance are the idea that we have to do something so we try harder, we effort, we attempt to control the ball rather than swing freely. These mental factors create a sense of struggle and often result in a very mechanical swing as we think about how we "should" swing.

Ultimately, these mental and emotional roadblocks create a lot of stress. Rather than help our performance, they actually interfere and take the fun and magic out of the game. The idea of letting go and getting out of the way is a difficult concept for some people to grasp. An example might be helpful here. One of my clients shared this story with me. He was playing in a tournament and not doing his best. His father, who had been an avid golfer with a scratch handicap, had passed away a few years earlier. With seven holes left to play, this man looked up towards the heavens and mentally reached out to his father. He said, "I thought you had more pull up there!" He related to me that he instantly felt a sensation in his spine and lightness in his body. He then birdied the next seven holes!

He reported to me that when he was able to play without expectations, with attachment to the outcome, he knew the ball was going on the green and into the hole. He continued, "The lie did not matter. It did not matter if I had to draw it, fade it, whatever...the ball was going on the green!"

This is a different kind of game. Golf at this level is not played from the mind and is not a matter of technique. This game is know by a relatively few people on the planet.

The system of Asthanga Yoga or Raja Yoga is designed to clear away the underbrush, so to speak, as allow access to the essential Self. The following chapters will discuss this process and its application to golf.

CHAPTER 2

Right Action
Yama and Niyama

You mean I am not supposed to lie about my handicap?
Sports Do Not Build Character...They Reveal It
—*John Wooden*

Golf is built on a history of integrity, honor and character. There are rules that create order, direction and structure. It is up to each individual to honor the rules of the game and play with dignity and respect. If you have too many clubs in your bag, it is up to you to take the penalty. If you move the ball, you call it. You are responsible to accurately record and report your final score. If you lose your ball in the woods, do you call it or drop one when no one is looking?

Yoga philosophy believes that we are ultimately responsible for what we create in life. "What we sow, so shall we reap." The law of karma suggests that there is a mathematical balance to life and our actions create causes for future results or consequences.

Five hours is a long time to devote to anything. It is most of a day. The time spent on the course can create a sense of well-being, contentment and joy or a huge amount of frustration, stress, disappointment and misery. It is really up to us what we do with the time and how our attitude and behavior affect our game.

First there are the *yamas* and *niyamas*. They provide the moral foundation for a spiritual life. Their practice brings the body and mind into harmony with the divine laws of nature and creates a sense of inner well-being. Yogananda in his interpretation of the Bhagavad Gita suggests, *"Breaking the rules of moral conduct creates not only present misery, but long-lasting karmic effects that bind the devotee to suffering and mortal limitation."*[1]

The yamas are: nonviolence, nonlying, nonstealing, nonattachment, and nonsensuality.

The niyamas are: purity of body and mind, contentment, austerity, self-discipline, self-study, and devotion to God.

Yamas

Nonviolence: Do you go into reaction over a poor shot? Do you break or throw your clubs, shout obscenities, or yell at others in your foursome? Do you make a big divot and leave it, not caring about the next player behind you? Do you ignore the ball marks on the green because you are too lazy or too self-centered to take the time to repair them?

Every hole you have an opportunity to create peace and harmony around you or do violence to nature and disrespect every other person on the course. In addition, your ability to stay calm, focused and positive, keeps you on your game.

Nonlying: Have your ever played with a real sandbagger? Someone who inflates their handicap so they will get lots of strokes in competitive play? If so, you know how disgusting it is to play under such conditions of dishonesty and deceit. If you lie, you ultimately cheat yourself, because it is impossible to respect yourself if you are dishonest. Word usually gets out around the club and people will not respect you either. It does not take long for your character to be revealed in this game.

Nonstealing: It seems like a no-brainer to realize you should not steal clubs from those on the course. Although on a public course your really have to watch your equipment. However, there are more subtle aspects to this principle. Have you ever been without someone who takes away the pleasure and joy of winning from another? They go to the tee even though someone else had the best score on the previous hole. They say, "You were just lucky" after you make a great shot or sink a long putt. They talk while you are ready to hit your ball. In a sense, this kind of behavior steals the opportunity for you to enjoy the game. Behind this behavior is selfishness and lack of consideration for the other. It is often overlooked as "kidding" between men.

Nonattachment: The concept of nonattachment is central to peace of mind, acceptance and emotional stability. Most of our upsets on and off the course result from unfilled expectations. If we hold some idea about how life is supposed to unfold, we typically have some strong emotional reaction when it is different. Our emotional reaction leads to breakdown and usually another bad swing and more trouble.

Some of the best high school golfers I have coached had trouble with anger management. They would mishit a shot and be upset. They had some idea or expectation that did not materialize. Golf is a funny game and a birdie can come out of the strangest circumstances.

How many times have we watched Tiger Woods hit a tee shot into the woods, only to recover with a great shot and make birdie. He was not yelling, screaming and breaking clubs. He went to the ball and made a great recovery shot.

I play at MoutainGate Country Club in Los Angeles. The 9th hole on the South course is rated as one of worst holes in California. It is a severe dogleg left, long par five that raps around a mountain. The entire slop slides to the right and any shot in the middle of the fairway runs off to the right side.

I was in a tournament and tried to cut the edge of the fairway on the left. I pulled the shot and hit it right into the side of the mountain. Only by the grace of God did my ball bounce off the mountain back into the fairway. I got lucky and was still in the hole. It was thrown back onto the course this side of the turn, but I had no clear shot left. I had to just get it over the corner and back in play. I hit a 7 wood, which left me 220 yards from the green. It was a blind uphill shot to the green. I now need the shot of my life. I made a good swing and hit a 3 wood 10 feet from the pin. I made the putt for a birdie!

Nonattachment may be the most difficult concept for most people to grasp. It does not mean that you do not care or that you do not try. It means that you accept what life brings to you. You do your best and let go of the outcome. You let go of your personal idea and stay open to other possibilities. This attitude allows you to stay open and receptive to life's unexpected turns and be ready to respond with all of your resources, physical and mental.

Nonsensuality: The outer interpretation of this precept is typically directed at sexuality, but there is much more to nonsensuality than meets the eye.

Paramahansa Yogananda, the founder of the Self Realization Fellowship, explains the deeper purpose of Kriya Yoga in his writings. The reader can find a more extensive discussion on this topic in my book, *Sacred Healing: Integrating Spirituality with Psychotherapy.* He provides a deeper insight into Sankhya yoga philosophy and the subtleties of life force energy. He suggests that when our attention is directed outward through our five senses (hearing, sight, touch, smell, and taste) our consciousness is grounded in physical, material reality and the delusion of our separateness from Spirit. In this typical psychological state of normal functioning, the life force energy is stabilized around the more primitive brain stem, which results in more automatic, biologically programmed reactions to threat and external stimuli. The flight or fight response is biologically located in brain stem, this more primitive aspects of the structure.

Kriya Yoga, which is an advanced form of pranayam (life force control) withdraws the life force energy into the spine and redirects its flow into the higher centers of the brain. As the life force energy is withdrawn from the outer senses and brought up to the Ajna center (spiritual eye located in the forehead), higher levels of awareness are activated.

Sankhya yoga philosophy discusses two mind states: *buddhi* and *manas. Buddhi* is a higher level of discriminative intellect that corresponds with the soul and *manas* is the normal psychological condition that exists when the life force energy is directed through the five senses.

Kriya yoga directs the life force energy to more internal subtle currents in the spine and brain and thereby awakens the buddhi nature in the higher centers of the brain. The result is greater clarity, more focus and a reduction in emotional reaction.

Limbic System

Reticular Activating System

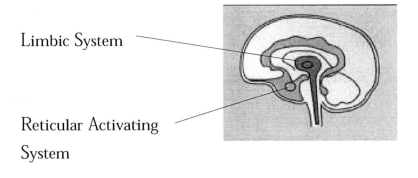

The RAS resides in the brain stem and controls waking consciousness. It iis intimately involved in the regulation of the sleep-waking cycle, arousal, and attention. It automatically regulates what information comes into our awareness. Imbedded within the RAS is the Pons Varolii: part of the brain stem—situated above the medulla and centered below the two hemispheres of the cerebrum – connecting the cerebrum, cerebellum, and medulla. Yogic science suggests that the Pons Varolii is the subtle magnetic pole turned outward toward the world of matter, which physiologically is every busy with sensory coordination. Advanced meditative practices redirect the flow of life force energy and awareness to higher centers in the brain so we can perceive more.

Picture by Bodyworks CD-ROM, Software Marketing Corporation

Application of Nonsensuality to Golf: The practical application for golf is actually quite profound. Most golfers tend to go into emotional reaction rather quickly. The average golfer tends to be overly mechanical in his/her approach. There is a tendency to think too much and lose touch with a more intuitive, feeling approach to the game.

There is a simple pranayam technique that is designed to internalize the flow of the life force energy into the spine. This breathing technique can be done as part of a pre-shot routine. It will shift brain activity into the right hemisphere, which increases one's ability to visualize, enhances the feeling, intuitive functions and reduces emotional reactions.

Chapter 4 discusses this technique in detail and how to do it. The CD *Find the Zone: Master the Mental Game of Golf* also provides instruction on this method.

Niyamas

The *niyamas* are: purity of body and mind, contentment, austerity, self-discipline, self-study, and devotion to God.

Purity of Body and Mind: The yogic emphasis on a pure body and mind is designed to keep the "instrument" clear for the divine presence. A pure body that is free from toxins and disease allows one to attend to higher interests beyond physical survival.

The pure mind allows for higher thoughts of divine perception and the attunement with more uplifting vibrations. A troubled mind that is filled with perversity and negativity creates enormous distractions that make it impossible to obtain the peace and bliss of meditation.

Application for Golf: The relationships to golf should be quite obvious. A body that is filled with impurities (i.e. toxins and disease) does not make for a good golf swing. Needless to say, it might be impossible to even swing if the body is in too much trouble. Recently, the good players have come to embrace the importance of physical conditioning. Gone are the days when a golfer can be forty pounds overweight and compete with the best. Modern PGA tour players, even those on the Champions tour like Gary Player, are hitting the gym and keeping physically fit. Many are actually turning to hatha yoga as a way to obtain both flexibility and strength.

The golf swing puts so much strain on the back that physical flexibility and stamina are important if one wants to play this game for life. Freddie Couples is a great example of how a poor back can derail a talent and a successful career. For several years his bad back kept him for playing well. Only recently at the Shell Houston Open did he finally return to the winner's circle. In a post game interview on the golf channel he thanked Butch Harmon for getting him back on track. Butch told Freddie that his swing was terrible. "He looked like a guy trying not to hurt his back!" Freddie recommitted to playing the game without the fear of hurting his back. He found his swing and won! Freddie said winning is great for the back!

Furthermore, diet also has a lot to do with the clarity of one's body and mind. More athletes are being more attentive to nutrition on and off the course. It is impossible to play well when the blood sugar is so low that the body does not have the energy to perform. Also lots of caffeine or alcohol do not make for championship play.

The body and mind work together. Stress starts in the mind and then shows up in the body. Purity of mind also refers to what kinds of things you are thinking. Love and respect are healing and empowering. Disrespect, disgust and anger are debilitating and undermine one's sense of power and well-being.

Contentment: The yogic prescription to develop an attitude of contentment provides a foundation for Self Realization. The non-dualistic teachings of Ramana Maharshi suggest that any separation created by the mind undermines our ability to live in our essential state of oneness. All too often, the spiritual seeker believes that the goal of realization is "out there" in the future or unattainable in this lifetime. When the mind lives in separation, then the focus is upon the technique to the degree that one continues to reaffirm the separation from the goal due to the constant "striving to obtain" realization. It is only by fully accepting each moment, accepting one's present condition regardless of circumstance can realization be obtained. Contentment suggests acceptance, a lack of "ego striving," and the ability to "be with" each moment of existence without preconceived ideas from the ego mind being superimposed on the experience itself.

In 1980 I spent a month in India. I was quite surprised to see the joy and light emanating from the eyes of those living on the street. The poorest of the poor were radiating an incredible joy, which was obviously not the result of their physical, material condition.

During that trip I had the opportunity to spend a week with Satya Sai Baba, considered to be a fully realized and liberated Being by his followers. He has demonstrated great spiritual powers to heal others and help awakening humanity. At the end of the week when I was preparing to leave, one of his devotee's spoke to me and said, "You have to be bold with Baba. Demand for what you want!" I thought maybe he is right. That afternoon as I sat in his presence, I began to mentally demand that he transmit some type of cosmic conscious experience to me. I figured this guy could do it. He certainly had the gift and the touch. Here I was in India. All my contentment was gone as I was having an internal temper tantrum demanding for some spiritual experience. A thought crossed my mind after about 30 minutes of this internal insanity. "If Baba could transmit this experience to me and he was not, maybe this is not the right time for it to happen. Maybe it will happen when it will happen and there is nothing I can "do" to make it happen." I left that afternoon gathering with a greater sense of peace and a fuller acceptance of my life than I had experienced in years.

Application for Golf: Contentment and Peak Performance: Striving for excellence is a razor's edge. One the one hand it motivates us to improve, on the other it affirms that we are not happy with our present circumstance. Contentment may allow us to settle into ourselves so we can actually perform at our highest level.

A few months ago I was shooting in the mid 70's on a regular basis. I was only a few strokes away from scratch golf. A friend of mine who had played on the Senior Tour knew my game and said, "You know, you can make a lot of money on the senior tour playing scratch golf. You don't have to win to do well." He got me thinking. "Maybe I can take a few more strokes off my game and give myself a chance to qualify for a Champion Tour event." My brother suggested I see Eddie Merrins at the Bel Air Country Club. Eddie is a very respected man in the golf world. I called him and set up some times when we could meet. We met for a couple of months and really "worked hard" at "improving my swing." Mr. Merrins is a great instructor. I was now in the 80's on a regular basis: 82, 83, 86, and 88. The more I "tried" and the harder I "worked" the further away I got from my goal, scratch golf. After a couple of months I was reflecting on my game. I realized that greed has played some part in my decision to improve my game. I was not satisfied or content with my current state. I did not believe that I had the ability to play better and looked outside myself for help and direction, which sometimes can be very helpful. I decided to stop the lessons and be happy with any score in the 70's. My next two rounds were 76!

I also revisited my values. I know that I am doing my best when I am helping individual's become aware of expanded states of being. Professional golf was a fun idea, but it was not in alignment with my core values. I realized I was directing my energy in the wrong direction.

Don't get me wrong. I am a strong believer in technical ability and swing coaches. Mr. Merrins was great, he was not the source of my high score. I needed to back away in order to reconnect with my core values and natural approach to the game. I was thinking too much; thinking about my swing and thinking about a profession that was off track for me. Many of the things that Mr. Merrins showed me ultimately became integrated at a deeper level when I stopped trying so hard. Too much trying and thinking gets in the way of this process.

In summary, contentment gets the "striving" out of the way so the mind does not create a separation between you and the goal of peak performance. Contentment allows you to drop deeper into the present experience, relax and open to your innate capacity. Again, we have the paradox: be content in the moment and yet strive for something more.

I attended a golf program with Fred Shoemaker, the author of Extraordinary Golf, a few years ago. Fred has a similar philosophy about golf given his Transcendental Meditation background. He has worked with PGA Tour professionals to help them correct swing problems. His method is based upon awareness training. He encourages the player to simply be aware of his/her body and feel the swing, simply notice what is happening. Inherent in this approach is a total acceptance and the ability to be perfectly content with the swing in that moment while the intention is to move to another level. Time and time again, the swing would transform just from awareness and intention. There was no "doing," no swing analysis, nor any mechanical evaluation.

Austerity: The attempt to discipline the body through rigorous physical austerities is a rather extreme practice. One gets images of a yogi holding his arm up for years. The underlying attempt to withdraw one's identification away from the body can be achieved with more advanced techniques such as Kriya Yoga where the life for energy is internalized through the breath and visualization processes.

Application for Golf: At first glance it might seem difficult to relate the practice of austerity to golf. However, it is my observation that most golfers quickly think about buying new equipment when their game is going south. If we think of the clubs as an extension of the body, then the practice of austerity might be very appropriate here. Rather than feed the delusion that the clubs are the source of the problem; one might wait and attend to deeper issues affecting his/her game. The ability to maintain the self-discipline to hold back the impulse to focus on outer manifestations of the game, ie., equipment, might yield greater learning at a deeper level.

I would even apply this concept to mechanical lessons. I have seen golfers who have a very negative attitude towards life struggle on the course. Their mental negativity creates considerable apprehension, self-doubt, physical contraction and lack of fluidity. The pattern with these individuals is to avoid taking an honest look at their mental approach to life and the game, and think it is a mechanical problem.

Once again, the ability to restrain the impulse to go to the surface of the body, and find the wisdom to deepen one's exploration into internal factors could yield surprising success.

Self-discipline: It is no secret that self-discipline is the key to self-mastery. This fact has been understood for thousands of years. Laziness does not yield great rewards. Any system that requires a honing of one's skills or one's perception must be taken seriously and performed on a regular basis. Advanced yogic training requires daily meditation practice and a lifetime commitment to learn to remain conscious in every moment.

Paramahansa Yogananda speaks about the process of self-realization and says that the disciple can have fifty percent of the work done through God's grace. Another twenty-five percept through the guru's grace, and the final twenty-five percent must come from the one hundred percent effort of the disciple.

Self-discipline requires a strong will and the ability to preserve over time. Most success stories contain episodes of great trials and tribulations. Jesus was tested for forty days and forty nights. One must never give up!

Application for Golf: Self-discipline is obviously related to peak performance in any sport. If you really want to improve your game, you have to practice and you have to consistently use the methods that are available to refine your practice routine, incorporate your pre-shot routine, and maintain good judgment for successful course management.

Self-discipline also applies to the rest of your life. If you let your diet go, stop exercising and drink too much, your game will suffer. If you lose touch with your values and stop living a life based upon honesty and integrity, your conscience will bother you and guilt will ruin your ability to win.

Personal development takes a lot of self-discipline. It is easier to avoid honestly looking at oneself. It takes a lot of courage to confront the emotional wounds that have caused pain and suffering in life. It is the way we respond to these early traumas that our capacity for maximum flexibility and adaptability. Peak performance requires freedom from inner conflicts.

For example, a young woman who was playing on the Futures Tour, the LPGA development tour, came to see me for a consultation. I asked her about her game and she told me the following story. "I was playing well in my last tournament and my caddie gave me the line on a putt. I did not trust him so I did what I thought was right. I missed the putt and then was really mad because I did not listen him. I just did not trust him."

I suggested she might have some issues about trust. She responded, "What do you mean?" This young woman really did not understand what was going on here. I said, "Well, you told me you did not listen to your caddie, who you paid, because you did not trust him." She again responded, "What do you mean?" I then asked about her relationship with her parents. She began to tell me about her mother and spent the next twenty minutes sobbing over her sense of abandonment. At the end of this time, I again suggested that she might want to.resolve her feelings with her mother because they appear to be affecting her game. She again responded, "What do you mean?" She never came back for another session. I have not seen her on the LPGA Tour.

For those who strive to win in the game at the highest level of competition, it is not good enough just to be good. One's inner life cannot be ignored. In the throes of competition, everything rises to the surface. Self-discipline can help you develop the skills to self-manage the intensity of mental and emotional factors that will impair your ability to play your best.

Self-study: The yogic directive for self-study refers to introspection in order to understand one's tendencies, both positive and negative. Ego consciousness is best transformed through awareness. Love and understanding provide the best environment for change. Isn't is true that children flourish in a loving environment and flounder in a hostile, negative approach that creates fear, shame and an inability to honestly express one's true nature? It is the same with personal development. Self-study, embraced in a non-judgmental, loving manner, allows one to recognize and trust innate character strengths and identify aspects of the ego that need to change.

Application for Golf: Golf is no exception. Learning about one's game must occur in a loving environment. After a bad shot I often ask a player, "What were you thinking and feeling just before you hit the ball?" If they are busy berating themselves they haven't a clue. Once he/she stops that wasted activity and actually begins to pay attention, i.e. self-study, then she/he has some valuable information for change.

It is only through introspection and awareness that we can improve. Mindlessly hacking away at balls on the range might be good exercise, but it won't do much to improve your golf game.

Devotion to God: Devotion is a central quality in the path towards Self Realization according to Paramahansa Yogananda. He states in his teachings that devotion is the magnet that draws God's response to the devotee. He advises us that since God created the Universe and has everything; God needs only one thing, our love. God gave us free choice and therefore, we must willing give our love to God.

Devotion is a matter of the heart and it is an act of selflessness. The actions that we dedicate and the love we give to another can open us to greater levels of awareness. Acts of devotion can be selfless if do them as a way to serve others, thereby creating good karma. Acts of devotion to serve God, when we have taken our desires and attachments out of the picture, deepen our capacity to live from our higher nature rather than our ego centeredness.

Finally, devotion deepens our capacity to be in tune with the Divine will. Although this does not guarantee that life will be easier, it does create more joy and a greater sense of meaning and purpose.

Application for Golf: Although many golfers, professionals and amateurs like, may not consider their actions as acts of devotion, I suggest they are. Millions of dollars are generated by the PGA tour every year for charities around the country. PGA professionals provide golf clinics through the First Tee organization to help inner city kids. Tiger Woods set up a foundation in order to give back to the community. Every local golf course around the country has golf benefits in which local players contribute to help non-profit organizations. The list goes on and on.

There are other ways that we can bring a devotional attitude to this game as well. Each time we play we often are paired with people that we do not know. We have at least four and a half hours together before the round is finished. You might consider holding the space that you may be of service to the people in your foursome. Perhaps just listening to their life story could be helpful. The magic of intention reveals itself when we consciously decide to align with some higher principle. Just try it. Before your next round, make a selfless decision that your time on the course could be helpful to someone you meet and see what happens.

Golf is such a great game because it does hold to possibility to meet people from all walks of life that open doors to many possibilities. When we see ourselves as an instrument for the Divine, then any place, on or off the course, can hold the possibility for service.

CHAPTER 3

Right Posture
Asana

Strength does not come from physical capacity. It comes from an indomitable will.
—Mahatma Gandhi

Asana becomes the next step in the yogic process. The physical postures or *asanas* allow one to stretch the spine, which allows for the subtle currents of energy to flow freely during *pranayama* and meditation practice. The postures also allow for tension that has been stored in the body to be released, which explains why this practice has become so popular and useful in stress-reduction programs. When *asanas* are taught correctly, in combination with the breath, the student begins to experience how breath effects the physical body: tension and chronic muscle contractions begin to dissolve as one consciously breathes into the source of discomfort.

Asana practice prepares the student for meditation, both mentally and physically. The mind begins to be drawn within as the focus of attention through the breath is placed upon the body. As the body becomes relaxed, and the flow of subtle energy is re-directed inward.

The *asana* system also relates to recent findings in mind-body medicine. Clinical observation with those patients receiving bodywork reveals that repressed memories and strong emotions are released when physical blocks in deep tissue are released. The unconscious also resides in the body. Specific systems of modified *hatha yoga* practice such as Phoenix Rising Yoga Therapy, use the power of *asana* to help release deep emotional conflicts. The body often provides a quicker path for emotional release and personal transformation than traditional psychotherapy techniques that focus mainly upon emotional and conceptual levels.

This aspect of Raja Yoga, Hatha Yoga, is becoming very popular with professional golfers. There are yoga classes in every city and hatha yoga is a great way to develop both strength and flexibility, which makes it ideal for golf.

There are a variety of postures in the system of Hatha Yoga. Below are some that specifically apply to the golf swing. In addition, hatha yoga is very good for the upper and lower back. A consistent practice can help to eliminate the golf injuries that often occur due to the constant turning and stress that is placed on the back. Futhermore, golf tends to be a one sided sport. Right handed golfers placed a lot of strain on the right side, which is seldom counter-balanced by left-sided

44

movement. Hatha yoga addresses balance and cross-lateral movement which helps to reduce the potential damaging effects of the golf swing.

Address

The proper address to the ball requires extension and flexibility in the hamstrings, the ability to rotate the spine, and stretch the lateral muscles along the rib cage. The golf swing tends to place a load on the lower back.

It addition to strength and flexibility, balance is a key factor in executing an effective and powerful swing. Without proper balance, all the power associated with the coil is lost and balls usually end up going left or right with significant loss of distance.

The system of hatha yoga is ideally designed for the golf swing because it provides all three physical prerequisites for a good swing: flexibility, strength and balance.

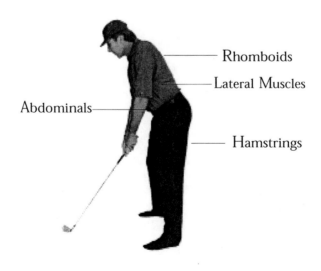

Rhomboids

Lateral Muscles

Abdominals

Hamstrings

ALIGNMENT AND EXPECTATIONS

The first thing we need to do is to make a proper alignment of your "yoga performance" expectations. As we have
discussed, hatha yoga is ideal for developing strength, balance
and flexibility. However, the deeper message of *The Yoga of
Golf* is to play from a deeper place within that accepts you as
really are. If you push yourself too far, too soon, you can hurt
yourself.

DO YOU EXPECT TO DO THIS?

If the answer is YES, then you probably go to the course and expect to play like Tiger Woods, Ernie Ells or Annika Sorenstam. We need to have a serious talk unless you are a PGA Tour player; in which case I hope you are playing like Tiger, Ernie and Annika.

Suzanne Strachan is a very advanced yoga instructor. She has successfully integrated great strength, balance and flexiblity in her work. She did not accomplish this in a week!

Hatha Yoga is helpful to anyone at any level. Like golf, it is non-competitive. You are working with yourself at your own pace. If you push too hard, you will damage yourself. I do not want to hear from your lawyer. Be conscious of what your body is able and willing to do.

Here are the keys to maximzing your hatha yoga routine:

- Challenge yourself, but DO NOT strain.
- Respect that every day your body is different depending upon how much golf you played the day before. Pay attention to what is true for you each day.
- Do not rush.
- Consciously use your breath with every movement.
- Move to the edge of tension. DO NOT PUSH. Stay at the edge and breathe into the tension. Your body will release and you will naturally move deeper into the pose.

WARM UP ROUTINE
Sitting Poses:
Cat Stretch1

This will help to warm up your body and back.

- Support yourself on your hands and knees.
- Gently, using your entire body, lean forward and continue moving to your right, or clockwise, circling back to where you began.
- Gentley reverse and move in the other direction.
- Repeat three to six times in each direction. Start on your more relaxed side.

Cat Stretch 2

This will help to warm up your body and back.

- Support yourself on your hands and knees.
- Gently round your back, inhale and pull in your abdomin, tucking your hips underneath.
- Gently lift your head, pulling your shoulders back, sending your sit bones up to the ceiling to arch your back.
- Move in and out of this posture six times.

Child's Pose

This pose will help to stretch out your back and arms.

- Begin on your hands and knees, sit back on your heals, extending your arms forward, or place them behind you, whichever is more comfortable.
- Breathe into your lower back and let yourself sink into your thighs. Hold the pose for six to eight deep breaths.

- If it is painful to sit back on your heels, then place a blanket on your calves and sit back.

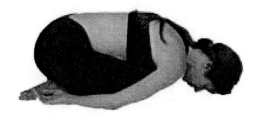

Knee to Chest Rock

This will warm up your back for further stretching

- On your back, hold behind your knees and gently pull towards your chest.
- Gently roll forward and backwards along your spine. Push off and use your momentum to return to the orginal position. Keep moving so you don't get stuck on your back.
- Roll back and forth six to eight times.
- Use a soft surface like a yoga mat or blanket to cushion the surface for your spine.

Hip Opener

This will help open your hips.

- Sit on the floor and pull your feet into your groin.
- Hold your feet and gently pull your feet inward and upwards. This movement will help your knees fall towards the floor.
- Hold for six to eight breaths.
- If you feel any knee strain, use a folded blanket under your legs and kness.
- If you feel any pain, or strain to your knees or hips: STOP!

Torso Rotation

This will warm up your back, spine and shoulders

- Stand with your feet at least shoulder width apart.
- Twist your body from left to right, letting your arms extend as you move from side to side.
- Exhale as your turn.

STANDING POSES
Standing Forward Bend

This will stretch your back, neck, shoulders and hamstrings.

Any forward bend can place extra strain on your disks. If you have any disk problems, consult your doctor or health professional before you try this pose.

- Stand with your feet shoulder width apart.
- Inhale as your extend your arms up and over your head.
- Exhale as you elongate your spine as you bend over to reach towards the floor.
- Soften your knees if it helps you get closer to the floor.
- Roll yourself up bringing your hands and arms overhead and then bring your hands to your side.
- Do this six times.

Warrior I

This will strengthen your legs, back, shoulders and arms. Good for the hips too.

- Standing straight up inhale and step forward with your right foot and raise your hands over your head.
- Exhale and bend your front knee at a right angle over your ankle.
- Keep your hips forward towards your front foot.
- Inhale and straighten your leg back to the original position.
- Repeat three times.
- Hold in the second position with your knee bent for six breaths.
- Inhale and return to standing.
- Repeat on other side.

Triangle

Good pose to stretch the back, flex the spine, stretch the hamstrings.

- Stand with feel wider than shoulders.
- Inhale and raise arms parallel to the floor.

- Exhale and bend forward, extend your hips to the right, placing your left hand or fingers on the floor or a block inside your left foot. Keep your outside edge of both feet and large toes pressed into the floor.

- Inhale look up turning your head and extend your right hand to the ceiling.

- Exhale, look towards the floor and inhale and look back up. Do this three times.

- To avoid needing another person to get you out of this position do the Following: Bend your right knee, push into the floor, and extend your left arm up as you straighten your leg and return to a standing position.

- Repeat on the other side.

Standing Forward Bend

A good routine will balance the body. After moving to the side or twisting, it is good to fold the body. Thus, we suggests another standing forward bend at this point. Refer to page 55 for directions.

Willow

Good for stretching lateral side of the body and stretches the spine.

- Stand with feet at shoulder width.
- Inhale and raise your right arm above your head.
- Exhale, pull your naval to your spine, tighten your buttocks, and extend your hip to right right as your body moves left.

- Move in and out three times and then hold for six breaths.
- Repeat on other side.
- Remember to breath as a way to relax into the pose. Inhale as you extend hip to hand, exhale give the up a gentle little push.
- Do not force the stretch.

Tree Pose

A balance pose that also strengthens the legs. Good for balancing both hemispheres of the brain as well.

- Stand with feet together.
- Inhale and place sole of right foot on the inside of your left thigh, as high as you can without straining, with toes pointing towards the ground.
- It helps to keep your eyes focused on a point in front of you to keep your balance.
- Bring your hands together as you pull your naval to your spine and tighten your buttocks.
- Hold for six breaths.
- Repeat on left side.
- Several variations are presented. Do the one that works best for you.

Level 1

Level 2

Tree Pose (continued)

Inside hints to keep from falling over:

- Keep joint of big toe and outside edge of foot pushed to the floor.
- Tighten the quad for stability.
- Press heel into your leg and relaxed your toes.
- Keep your head, hands and foot in a straight line.
- Extend up your spine as you breathe.

Level 3

62

LYING POSES
Corpse

An ideal pose of relaxation and transition between poses.

- Lay on your back with your arms at your side.
- Close your eyes.
- Tense your body in the inhale and fully relax on the exhale. Do this five times.
- Keep you palms up.
- Close your eyes and breathe, releasing all tension from the body. Do this for two minutes.

Yogic Crunch

Good for strength and abdominal muscles. These muscles are actually the front of your back. You need to have strong abdominal muscles for a healthy back.

- Lay on your back.
- Place your hands behind your head and support your neck.

Caution: Remember to keep your chin tucked towards your chest in order to avoid straining your neck.

Yogic Crunch (continued)

- Exhale, roll up as you lift your tail bone up to engage your abdominal muscles and firmly press your feet into the floor as you tighten your buttocks.
- Keep your elbows wide at your side.

- Also, you can twist to each side as you exhale and lift your knee to the opposite elbow. Remember to keep your foot pressed into the floor for leverage.
- Do as many as you like.

Lower Back Push Downs

Good for the abdomen.

- Lie on your back.
- Place your arms and hands at your side.
- Exhale, pull in your naval and tighten your buttocks.
- Push the back of your waist into the floor and tilt your hips upward. Hold the pose and inhale.
- Exhale and release.
- Repeat six times.

Hamstring Stretch

Great for stretching hamstrings. Helps to develop better golf stance with proper angles at address.

- Lie on your back.
- Place your hands behind your left thigh.
- Bend your left leg.
- Inhale, press your foot into the floor as you extend your leg.

- Exhale and relax as you lower your leg.
- Repeat three times.
- Extend your leg and hold it for six breaths.
- Bend your knee and lower your foot to the floor and relax. Breathe.
- Repeat on other side.

Bridge

Good for strengthening and stretching the back, hips and thighs.

- Lie on your back, bend your knees with feet flat on the floor.
- Place your arms at your side with your palms facing down.
- Inhale and left your pelvis as high as is comfortable. Do not push yourself if you have lower back problems.
- Exhale as you slowly lower, pulling your naval in and tightening your buttocks. This will allow you to articulate your spine achieving greater range and control as you come down.
- A variation includes synchronizing your arms with the lifting of your pelvis. Promotes good upper and lower body connection and timing.
- Repeat six times.

Seated One Legged Forward Bend

Good for stretching hamstrings and lower back.

Caution: Be careful if you have disk or lower back problems. Bending your knees will soften the pose and take the load off your lower back.

- Sit on the floor and extend your left leg.

- Inhale and extend from your back and raise your arms up over your head.

Seated One Legged Forward Bend (continued)

- Exhale and bend from the hips towards your foot.

- Keep your left leg as straight as possible and hold your thigh, calf or foot.
- Exhale to relax.
- Repeat three times up and down and then hold the pose for six breaths. Remember to breathe into the tension, don't strain or push yourself.
- Repeat on the other side.

To avoid disk compression, inhale to extend the spine and exhale to relax.

We have shown this pose using two props, a blanket and a rolled yoga mat, both help when the hamstrings are tight. The blanket lifts the coccyx, and in conjunction with the slight bend in the knee, allows for isolation of the hamstrings.

Seated Two Legged Forward Bend

Now repeat the process with both legs extended.

Cobra

Good for strengthening the lower back and arms, chest and shoulders. This posture is especially helpful for lower back problems involving disk compression.

- Lie on the floor face down.
- Separate your legs to ease strain on your lower back.
- Place your elbows underneath your shoulders at a right angle.
- Keep your elbows close to your body.
- Exhale and pull your navel back into your spine while tightening the buttock muscles.
- Inhale, pull your upper torso forward, remember to keep your abdominals pulled up into your spine and your buttocks tight. Pull your shoulders back.
- Exhale and lower yourself to the floor.
- Repeat six times. Remember to breathe: Inhale as you come up and exhale going down.

Cobra Variation

If you have some lower back or disk problems, you might find it painful to push up into the full cobra. This variation creates less pressure on the lower back.

- Lie on the floor face down.
- Separate your legs to ease strain on your lower back.
- Place your elbows underneath your shoulders at a right angle.
- Keep your elbows close to your body.
- Exhale and pull your navel back into your spine while tightening the buttock muscles.
- Inhale, pull your upper torso forward, but keep your forearms on the floor. Remember to keep your abdominals pulled up into your spine and your buttocks tight. Pull your shoulders back.
- Exhale and lower yourself to the floor.
- Repeat six times. Remember to breathe: Inhale as you come up and exhale going down.

Loqust

This pose is good for strenthening the legs, buttocks, upper and lower back and conditoning.

- Lie flat on the floor face down.
- Position your arms along side your body with the palms down.
- Inhale, tightening your buttocks as you pull your shoulders and arms up and back, while extending out from your hips as you lift your legs. This will lift your trunk.
- Exhale and lower your trunk, head and arms slowly to the ground.
- Repeat four to six times.

Here is a variation for those with lower back problems: Follow the same steps as above, but keep your knees bent with upper thighs on the floor.

Downward Facing Dog

Good for strengthening arms and shoulders and can be used to stretch hamstrings.

- Begin in the child's pose with arms extended and toes curled under.
- Inhale, push away from the floor and extend into your entire back as you press your toes into the ground.
- Maintain the same back angle as you straighten your knees. This will send you hips up into the air.
- Let your head and neck relax.
- While holding the pose for three to six breaths, inhale as you push back and away from the floor and exhale as you try to relax.
- If you need to, soften your knees.
- Return to child's pose floor and relax.

Child's Pose

Salutation to the Sun

This sequence of postures is a great series because it has so many benefits for the golfer. It stretches the spine and hamstrings, increases dynamic energy, develops coordination between lower and upper body, and is aerobic for conditioning.

There are many steps, so we will proceed one at a time:

Stand at the front of your mat and place your hands together in front of your heart with your fingers pointing upward. Begin with an inhale and then exhale.

Inhale and extend from your spine upward into your arms and hands .

Exhale, bend from the hips. sweeping your arms back as you bend your knees and lift your tail bone back and up. Place your fingers or hands as close to the floor as possible. If necessary, bend your knees.

On the inhale, step back with your right foot and bend your left knee. Keep your left knee over your ankle at a right angle.

On the exhale, step back with your left foot to a plank or push up position. If you need to, rest your kness on the floor.

On the exhale, move your kness, chest and chin to the floor, keeping your buttocks raised.

Inhale, slide forward, keeping your navel pulled in towards your spine, and draw yourself upward bringing your shoulders down. Arch your back as you push up with your hands and forearms.

If you can't do this variation, do the one with your elbows down, keeping the navel pulled up.

Bend your elbows as you bow forward, exhale and push back onto hands and knees (cat) and then lower into the child's pose. Hold for one breath.

Exhale, push back into the downward dog. Push back with your hands, lift your tail bone to the ceiling and keep your shoulders down.

Inhale and step forward and through with your right foot. Position your knee above your ankle at a right angle. Keep your eyes stright ahead.

If you can't do this, place kness down to the floor in cat pose, and then step your foot forward.

On the exhale, bring your left leg up next to your right leg, and move into a standing forward bend. Place your fingers or hands on the floor and relax your neck handing down.

Roll up your spine and lift your arms upward to a standing position. Bring your arms even with your ears and allow your eyes to look foward.

On the exhale, bring your arms down and your hands in front of your heart. Remain for one full breath.

Repeat this series four to six times.

Seated Spinal Twist

This pose strengthens the abs and promotes spinal flexiblity for rotation.

- Sit on the floor and bend your right leg.
- Bend your left leg, crossing over your right.
  Make sure both hips are on the floor.
- Place your right arm over and around your left leg.
  Hug your leg on the exhale.
- Place your left hand behind you on the floor.
- Push your hand and foot into the floor as you inhale and extend up your spine.
- Exhale as your turn to your left and look back. Move your shoulder blade into your spine to increase the rotation. As you inhale, push into the floor and extend up your spine.
- Hold for two to four breaths.
- Unwind and repeat on other side.

Lying Leg Twist 1

Good stretch for your lower back, abdomen, chest and shoulders. Two variations are shown here.

- Lie flat on your back with your knees bent and feet flat on the floor.
- Extend both arms straight out from your sides.
- Turn your head to the left side.
- Keep your shoulders on the floor and rotate both legs with knees bent to the right side of your body.
- Move back and forth three times.
- Breathe into the tension and hold for four to six breaths.
- Unfold and rest for three breaths.
- Repeat on the other side.

Lying Leg Twist 2

Good stretch for your lower back, abdomen, chest and shoulders.

- Lie flat on your back with your knees bent and feet flat on the floor.
- Extend your right arm straight out from your side.
- Keep your shoulders on the floor and extend your left leg and bend your right knee over your body to your left side.
- Exhale and turn your head to the right side to look at your arm. As you inhale, look back to the ceiling. Move your head back and forth three times.
- Breathe into the tension and hold for two breaths.
- Unfold and rest for two breaths.
- Repeat on the other side.

Caution: if you can't get your knee to the floor, please place a folded blanket under your leg.

Corpse Pose

An ideal pose of relaxation and transition between poses. This is the last pose for your practice.

- Lay on your back with your arms at your side.
- Close your eyes.
- Tense your body in the inhale and fully relax on the exhale. Do this five times.
- Keep you palms up or down.
- Close your eyes and breathe, releasing all tension from the body. Do this for two minutes. Imagine your body filled with light.

CHAPTER 4
Life Force Control
Pranayama

*Do not dwell in the past, do not dream of the future, concentrate the
mind on the present moment.*
—*Buddha*

Pranayama is the scientific practice of controlling the
life-force energy through the direction and use of the breath.
The yogic key to self-realization is the transmutation of the
life force energy by withdrawing the life force and redirecting
it up the spine into the higher centers of the brain. The breath
is the means to accomplish this.

As we previously discussed, the ultimate goal of yogic
practice is union. This union is possible when consciousness
is no longer identified with the limited ego that experiences
itself as separate from the Divine. When the life force energy
is directed out through the five senses, ego consciousness is
predominant. By ego consciousness, we are referring to the
mental state of *manas,* the state where the rational mind is
attempting to control everything. In ego consciousness, life
seems like a constant struggle, the personal self tends to be
inflated, thinking it is responsible for all good and bad things

that happen. With regards to golf, the ego keeps us out of the Zone.

Advanced forms of *pranayama,* such as *kriya yoga,* work to cleanse the body of venous blood, so that the heart and lungs do not have to work so hard. Breath controls the flow of energy. Three subtle currents run along the astral spine: the *ida,* on the left, comes upward as one inhales, the *pingala,* on the right side of the astral spine, goes downward upon the exhale, and the *sushumna* is in the center of the spine. Advanced *pranayama* practice focuses the breath in the center of the spine in order to draw life force energy away from the outer senses into the higher centers of the spine and brain. Simply holding the breath will not achieve these results.

In deep states of meditation, once the heart has been stopped, it is possible to stop breathing for extended periods of time and cause no harm to the brain or any organs of the physical body. The body can be sustained on subtle energy during these altered states of consciousness.

There are a variety of yogic breathing techniques that are designed to balance the hemispheres of the brain and achieve inner stillness.

Alternate nostril breathing will balance the hemispheres. The left nostril effects the right hemisphere and the right nostril effects the left hemisphere. There are a number of ways to do this. The simplest method is to take your thumb on the right hand and gently close your right nostril. In hale through your left nostril to the count of eight. Now close your left nostril with the ring finger of the right hand and exhale to the count of eight. Now inhale through the right nostril to the count of eight and then exhale through the left nostril to the count of eight. You can do this technique for a couple of minutes prior to meditating.

The yogic techniques for the control of life force energy may be the most helpful practical techniques that yoga offers the golfer.

It is easy to tell someone to concentrate more, be in the present, quiet your mind, etc. However, it is my experience that most golfers do not know how to accomplish these things. Simply telling someone that they have to quiet their mind is quite useless unless you provide the technology to do so.

Yoga teaches us two different ways to breathe. One is through the nostrils and the other is through the mouth. Both are useful and have different results.

I have learned that nostril breathing is great for training and preparation, but is not the best method for peak performance during or right before competition because it tends to create more alpha states which are very mellow, very relax and too subdued. Nostril breathing is great in the morning and when you are meditating to learn how to disengage from you mind. I advise you not to do right before competition. I have had players tell me that feel too mellow and do not feel enough dynamic energy to complete.

Breathing through the mouth, on the other hand, provides a very grounded feeling and is solid and keeps you centered in competition.

We will discuss meditation in a future chapter, which will use nostril breathing.

All methods for enhancing deeper concentration and managing internal states employ the breath. Meditation, biofeedback, hypnosis, and yoga all make use of the breath. There are several reasons that the breath is so powerful.

First, the breath is closely linked to physiological states. When you learn to manage your breath, you can lower heart rate and lower blood pressure, which serves to reduce tension and stress. We know that too much tension and high arousal levels impair optimum performance in sports. Remember the benefits of proper breathing: decreased heart rate, decreased cardiopulmonary stress, decreased muscle tension, decreased fatigue, decreased need for sleep, decreased perception of pain, increased blood and oxygen to the brain and heart, alpha brain wave activation, and increased relaxation response.

Second, the breath serves as the technology to disengage from the mind. Many of the key points in this book relate to "not thinking" about outcome. A process-oriented approach that is centered from a deeper part of the self results in the best performance. Thinking about mechanics and future outcomes does not lead to great results.

The linear, rational mind is actually a more surface aspect of the self. It is similar to the difference between left and right brain activity. The left-brain is good for thinking and logical conclusion, and right brain is more effective in visual, kinesthetic and intuitive functions.

Focusing upon the breath actually helps you disengage from the left hemisphere and the linear, logical aspects of the brain. I recently watched my brain wave patterns while I was hooked up to a neurological biofeedback system. I spent about one minutes in a yogic breathing technique. The shift in the brain wave activity was striking: 90% of the brain wave pattern came from the right hemisphere.

Third, the breath is the key to unlocking a deeper perception of the self. Most people feel that they are defined by their thoughts, emotions and physical condition. Specifically, if they have a positive thought about themselves, then they feel good. If they have a negative thought about themselves, then they feel inadequate or lacking in some way. If they are emotionally uplifted, then they feel happy. If they feel down or in a mood, then they would say they are not good that day. In fact, these definitions of self are rather surface definitions.

There is a deeper self, a self we can call the essential self, which is more consistent and unaffected by the transitory thoughts and moods that pass through our consciousness. This deeper self is grounded in positive states of peace, joy, and love. It is possible to realize the deeper self and the "true self," and become less identified with the more surface aspects of our being. Once again, the breath is the key to this inner realization.

Fourth and finally, the tools of visualization are more powerful and more effective when you are in a deeply relaxed and focused state. The breath is the key to reaching that relaxed and highly concentrated state of mind. Use whatever method you like, meditation, biofeedback, yoga practice, or self-hypnoses. The key is to breathe, observe the breath and discover the deeper aspects of your nature that are innately peaceful, serene and joyful.

The Application to Golf: It is very simple. If you realize your essential self, you are less affected by the passing thoughts and emotions that arise to undermine your concentration, self-confidence, and enjoyment of the game. The easiest way to free yourself from those inner voices of doubt that say, "You're going to hit it in the lake," or "I can't hit this shot," or "Don't do.," is to actually have developed the inner discernment to know that you are more than those thoughts.

In addition, it is very difficult to achieve the state of internalization without re-directing the life force energy. It is impossible to develop greater concentration, a greater capacity for visualization, and a greater sense of feel for rhythm and tempo when you are focused on everything; all essential factors in enhanced golf performance.

On Course Breathing Technique

During the pre-shot routine, inhale and exhale evenly through your mouth. Imagine a current of energy in the middle of your spine coming up on the in-breath and going down on the out-breath. Pretend that your breath actually travels right up your spine to the middle of your forehead and then back down on the out-breath. This technique will shift more brain activity to your right hemisphere, which activate more visual and kinesthetic ability. It also pulls you out of your emotions very quickly. This technique will quiet your emotions and help you get out of left-brain thinking. You will feel more centered and have a greater ability to focus on your rhythm and time: keys to a good golf swing in the heat of competition. Remember to breathe evenly through the mouth.

This breathing technique can be done in a few seconds as you stand behind the ball and visualize your shot. It does not have to add extra time to your routine and will help you stay focused and calm.

CHPATER 5

Internalization of the Mind and the Senses

Pratyahara

The wise adapt themselves to circumstances,
as water molds itself to the pitcher.
Chinese Proverb

Internalization or *Pratyahara*, is reached when consciousness has been successfully redirected inward, away from the outer aspects of the five senses to the spine and higher centers in the brain. The previous pranayam or breathing techniques help to achieve this state. Superconscious perception is acheived as a natural result when the life force is redirected into the higher centers of the brain. The experience in this state is one of great peace, focus and calm

Our previous discussion about *manas* and *buddhi* is relevant here. As the life-force energy is redirected inward, consciousness can move into higher states of awareness. It is this state of internalization that allows the shift of awareness from *manas* (the sense mind) to *buddhi* (discriminative intellect). The discriminative aspect of the mind is achieved as the life force energy is internalized and drawn up to the higher center of the brain.

Kriya Yoga is an advanced technique that accomplishes this within a few minutes. This state of internalization is the doorway to deep meditation. It is important to remember that this state is achieved with little effort. It is the specific use of the breath, focused attention, visualization and intention that achieves the goal.

In summary, the internalization of consciousness is the by-product or result of life force control techniques. When the focus is on the breath and imagining the breath in the spine and moving up into the brain, then consciousness will follow where the attention is focused. Since the life force energy is withdrawn inward, away from the outer senses, the outer world is less apparent: outer sounds, smells, bodily sensations are greatly reduced.

The value for yogic practiced is that the life force energy, being directed into the higher centers in the brain through the spinal channels or currents, actually transmutes certain collected energies that impact behavior, habits, perception, and past tendencies. Practitioners of yoga often report profound changes in their thinking, moods and/or behavior as the result of these simple practices.

The health benefits of yoga are well documented. People have less visits to physicians, less hospitalization, lower rates of cancer and heart disease, improved raltionships with co-workers and higher rates of job satisfaction.

Application for Golf: The previous "on course breathing technique" is designed to draw the attention inward and create a more focused, internalized state of awareness.

To review, we have discussed how this shift in awareness through the breath will activate more right hemisphere activity thereby creating a greater ability for visualization, less mechanical swing thoughts, and a greater sense of feel for better rhythm and timing.

There is another benefit that the golfer achieves from this process: a greater internal focus with less distraction from outer stimuli.

Many golfers are too responsive and reactive to the people and noises around them. They hear everything: every little movement, every little whisper, airplanes flying overhead, golf carts passing by, birds chirping. It is a wonder they can play at all. I am amazed that a friend's wife can hear us whisper from thirty yards away when she is on the tee.

The greater the internal focus, the less you will hear. It is simple, as the life force energy becomes internalized; the outer senses are less activated. You will be more focused, concentrate more effectively, visualize better and have less negative mind-chatter affecting your swing. In addition, since putting requires a lot of attention, any outer distractions can move a good stroke off line.

We all know that the short game is where the money is. The old saying, "Drive for show and putt for dough" is true. The short game, chipping and putting, offers the best opportunity to take stroke off your game. Unfortunately, most average golfers do not practice their short game as much as they do their woods and irons. However, this shift in attending to consciousness, which will help the short game, might provide more interest in chipping and putting. This aspect of the game can become more meditative and does respond quickly to a more integrated mind/body connection and a greater sense of feel.

CHAPTER 6

Concentration

Dharana

The true value of a human being is determined primarily by the measure and the sense in which he has attained liberation from the self.

--Albert Einstein

Dharana, or concentration is the next factor to consider in the unfolding process of awakening. It is not enough to internalize consciousness without the ability to remain focused; otherwise the distracting and ever-perpetual thoughts of the mind will draw your attention from one place to another like a leaf floating on the breeze. You may have heard the expression, "monkey mind." It refers to the mind jumping from one place to another, like monkeys in the trees.

Once again it is unreasonable to think that through the will alone, we will be able to maintain focused concentration. The mind cannot control the mind. Our ability to concentrate is like a muscle that must be developed. Fortunately, there are several yogic techniques that are proven to enhance concentration.

Mindful Awareness Training:

Meditation is not a means to an end. It is both the means and the end.

First, simply observing the breath will shift the identification of self away from the ever-changing contents of the mind to the consciousness of awareness that is the observer. The technique is quite simple.

- Sit either on the floor or on a chair with your spine erect, shoulders relaxed and back and the chin parallel with the floor.
- Close your eyes and keep your gaze up through the center of your forehead.
- Breathe from the diaphragm.
- Allow your body to breathe on its own. Do not attempt to control the quality of breath.
- Breathe through your nostrils.
- Place your attention on the sensation of the breath as it comes in and out of the body.
- Simply observe the breath. If your awareness moves off the breath into thoughts, images, daydreams, etc., simply return your attention to the breath.
- Continue this practice as long as you like.

This creates a fundamental shift in the state of being that now becomes grounded in the deeper self that is not identified with the mind. A figure-ground reversal occurs and the thoughts of the mind are now seen as separate from the true self. The true or essential self is experienced as stable, peaceful, joyful and free from the effects of thought.

Mantra Meditation

Mantra (repetition of sacred formulae, or names of God) also becomes useful in this process because it allows one to focus upon a single-pointed object, in this case a sacred sound that carries a vibration of holiness.

Mantra is based upon the theory that certain languages such as Sanskrit and Hebrew are "seed" languages in that the sound of the word carries a vibration that actually changes consciousness. Therefore, mentally repeating a sound actually creates an inner vibration that transmutes consciousness into a higher state.

One example of a mantra is "So Hum". It means "I am He." Other mantras might be "Om Guru," "Ram, Ram, Ram," "I am Love, etc.

There is an ancient Tibetan chant, "Om Mani Padme Hum" that I personally like very much. It has been chanted for thousands of years and, therefore, has great spiritual power. The words Om (the cosmic sound of creation), Mani (Lotus), Padme (Jewel) have a powerful impact on consciousness. As we have discussed, certain sounds carry specific vibrations. This chant is one of them.

Mantra Technique:

- Synchronize your breath with the sound.
- As the breath comes in mentally repeat the first syllable of the mantra.
- As the breath goes out, mentally repeat the second part of the mantra.

Various Sanskrit *mantras* hold this power to fix the awareness on the sound and thought of the Divine.

As one develops the capacity to stay focused upon the breath and the *mantra,* then the distracting thoughts of the mind recede into the background of consciousness. This process allows one to observe the contents of the mind and the field of emotions that come and go across the screen of awareness. This practice deepens the awareness that one is not the body, mind, or emotions. One becomes more stabilized as the observer of pure consciousness.

This practice develops an inner strength that is laser-like in its focus. Deep concentration allows one to stay focused on the subtle aspects of consciousness, ie. peace, joy, love, and to rise above the distractions of the mind, body, and emotions.

Once we move into deeper states of concentration, the reality of the mind's creation becomes as tangible as the movies on the big screen. We observe our mind creating the images and realities that we hold so dear. We watch the dramas and stories emerging and dissolving into the void from which they come. Thus, our ability to concentrate becomes the tool for opening more deeply into a deeper state of awareness that is beyond the limited illusion of outer, material reality.

Application for Golf:

Overcoming negative mind chatter: Mastery of concentration in meditation has great benefit for the golfer. A major detrimental factor in a round of round is "negative mind chatter." All too often we begin to think, "Don't hit it in the water!" "Side hill lie, this is really impossible!" "Don't chunk it!" "Don't leave the putt short!" The dialogue goes on and on and it can get a lot worse. "You idiot, how could you do that!" "You stupid fool, why do you even waste your time playing this game?!" I suspect you have even heard worse than this on a tough day.

If you have a lot of negative chatter, you have probably found it difficult to just "stop" the inner distraction. You can't because the mind cannot stop the mind! However, the internalization and concentration techniques will stop the negativity and give you the internal ability to let that stuff go very quickly if it should arise.

Developing the observer: Once you have experienced the meditative state where you perceive that you are not the thoughts of the mind, it is easier to remain in an observer capacity and let that stuff move through your awareness, on and off the course. So, rather than resist the negative chatter on the course, you can simply be aware that it is there, take a breath, exhale and let your attention return to the task at hand. You will have a new ability to stay in the moment and not go into reaction from a passing thought arising in your mind.

Increased focus: Your improved capacity for concentration will also help you stay focused through your swing. Often I hear golfers tell me, "At the top of my back swing I just lost it. My mind jumped somewhere and I got distracted." Increased concentration skills will improve your game and take strokes off your score.

Many of the junior golfers I have seen have some degree of Attention Deficit Disorder. They just can't stay focused for very long. You can see their attention is jumping all over the place and negatively affects their game. This type of meditation training can help individuals overcome these types of challenges without the use of medication.

CHAPTER 7

Contemplation

Dhyana

If you can dream it, you can do it.
—Walt Disney

If your dreams turn to dust....vacuum.
—Unknown

It is a common misconception to believe that the purpose of meditation is to create a blank mind. I am not sure where this misconception developed, but it is not the goal of any form of yoga. Meditation and the greater system of Raja Yoga is designed to help the devote become one with God, however she/he chooses to conceive of God. Thus, the act of contemplation is designed to focus upon the goal, Divine percpetion and Divine union, once the consciousness has been internalized and focused in deep concentration.

The process of contemplation serves to take one even deeper into Divine union; because, "We become That which we contemplate." There is an old story of a disciple who was sent into a room and instructed by his Master to meditate on a water buffalo. Three days later, his master came to him and asked the disciple to follow him out of the room. The student protested that he could not get through the doors because his horns were too big!

The fact is we seem to follow where our mind goes. On a psychological level, it is well known that constant negative self-talk or internal dialogue undermines one's sense of self-esteem, self-worth and sense of well-being. If the internal dialogue is, "You are really stupid, ugly, fat, a loser," etc. you feel lousy. Maybe you can hide how you feel from others, but it will undermine your sense of self and ability to function successfully in the world. This is a form of contemplation. Here it is contemplation on the negative. Yoga teaches a system to contemplate on the positive!

Given the progression of consciousness, as the result of yogic practice, from the outer interests of everyday life to the inner world of more subtle perceptions, we now have developed the capacity to concentrate and focus. Therefore, we need to choose the object for contemplation. Since the yogi is going to sit for some time concentrating on some inner experience or phenomena, she/he must define the focus for contemplation. To repeat, the goal is not a blank mind, but a focused attention on the spiritual object of desire.

The spiritual discipline of yoga suggests that the devotee hold some aspect of God as the focus. This is where individual choice predominates. The devotee may conceive of God as Jesus, or Buddha, or Ram, or Divine Mother, or simply as

Light.   The wise student keeps a steady bead on the Divine. God becomes the polestar of the mind. The attention does not waver and the focus remains clear: God, God, God. These inner callings tug at the Divine heartstrings to capture a Divine response. Most typically, peace is the first experience of God. However, the Divine is also experienced as love, joy, and bliss.

The Bible says, "Be still and know that I am God." It is through this process of quieting the mind and opening to the inner stillness that the devotee becomes one with the Divine experience. The mind is never blank. The techniques of yoga that withdraw the life force within and focus the attention upon a specific aspect of God, create the shift in consciousness that allows for the deeper experience of God's love and peace.

Application for Golf:

Visualization: Although the yogic path is clearly designed for higher spiritual purposes, the process of contemplation is actually not that foreign to the advanced golfer, although he/she may not conceive of it in this particular manner. With regards to golf and peak performance, contemplation is very similar to visualization.

Visual and kinesthetic imagery: The purpose of visualization is to concentrate through both mental and kinesthetic means to obtain the desired goal. Successful visualization techniques actually function to create the desired goal: a drive in the middle of the fairway, a putt from thirty feel, a wedge next to the pin. Just as in the yogic process one's becomes the goal of contemplation, i.e, union with the Divine, the golfer becomes the successful performer.

Visualization techniques have been used for years with Olympic champions from all sports and all countries.

The mind has enormous power to affect the body. Scientists generally agree that we use only a small percentage of our actual brainpower. Research has been done regarding mind/body relationships and the results are striking.

Visual imagery appears to be one way that the power of the mind is directed. A visual image can be anything that captures the intention for the desired outcome. The mental image can be a real picture or something imagined.

Considerable research has done on the physical effects of mental imagery. These findings are important for sports psychology. Warner and McNeill, from the school of Medicine, at East Carolina University, reviewed hundreds of studies and reported that mental imagery can be used as mental practice to prepare oneself for athletic performance. They cited research that actually measured the muscle movements that occurred just from mental imagery. In other words, our muscles react to our thoughts. Thinking and imagining hitting a golf ball actually activates minute muscle movements that correspond to the kind of visualizations that we create. They discuss two ways to visualize an action. One way is to think about the action and create a visual image or picture of the process. We call this visual imagery. The other way is to create a kinesthetic sense or feeling of the action taking place. We call this kinesthetic imagery. Some people are more visual and others are more kinesthetic.

Mind/body research: The power of the mind and the impact of thought is also discussed in the research literature. Warner and McNeill noted that after Roger Bannister became the first person to run one mile in less than four minutes, 52 others accomplished the same feat within that year. What had been considered impossible was now possible. When one's belief system opens, then greater achievements seem possible. They suggest that it is unlikely that one's body will do more than one's mind believes is possible. Olympic athletes are taught to use creative imagination to help them obtain peak performance.

Some of the most powerful research that has been done on the mind-body connection comes from medical research. Carl Simonton, M.D. found that programs, which included attitudinal change, and visualization processes that used symbolic images, resulted in patients living longer than patients who did not incorporate these methods into their medical treatment. In addition, over twenty percent were able to cure themselves of terminal illnesses.

The evidence is clear that there is a tremendous connection between our mind and our body. The yogic methods are useful here because they enhance the power of visualization skills because consciousness is more focused, more concentrated and thereby more powerful. Yogic principles teach us that "energy follows thought." Visualization is a form of thought and we direct our energy, which orchestrates our behavior, through focused visualization.

Power of visualization: Todd Yoshitake, the head PGA Pro at Riviera Country Club, shot a 62 at a Q School event. He told me that he spent the previous evening visualizing every hole and every shot on the course. Much to his surprise the day unfolded just as he had visualized it the night before. This is a striking example of how powerful these techniques can be.

Preshot Routine: I am often surprised to find that many golfers of all levels do not have any consistent preshot rountine. They typically just set up next to the ball, look down the fairway, waggle, and hit the ball.

The preshot routine, encapsulates everything we have been discussing. In the few seconds before addressing the ball, the golfer has the opportunity to breathe, internalize one's energy, focus on the target, visualize the flight of the ball, and feel the best swing he/she has ever made.

The preshot rountine should be consistent with every shot. It provides the opportunity to let go of the mind, open to the deeper potential within, committ to the target, and imagine the miraculous. It is a moment to mentally affirm living in the Zone and open to the deeper trust of one's swing.

More specifically, here are the steps to developing a solid preshot routine:

1. Stand behind the ball.
2. Take 2-3 breaths with the "on course breathing technique " provided.
3. Pick a very specific target where you want the ball to land.
4. Visualize the flight of the ball landing on the target.
5. Create a kinesthetic memory of a great swing for that particular shot.
6. Focus on rhyth, timing, and tempo.
7. Allow any distracting thoughts to pass through your

awareness and bring yourself back to the moment.

8. Mentally affirm that you can make the shot.

This process should take less than 15 seconds. It should not slow down your game.

CHAPTER 8

State of Oneness

Samadhi

Your vision will become clear only when you look into your heart... Who looks outside, dreams. Who looks inside, awakens.
—Carl Jung

The ultimate purpose for the spiritual aspirant is to integrate his/her Divine realization into everyday life. It is not sufficient to have transcendtal experiences sitting on a meditation pillow, but be unable to ground those glimpses of the Divine into every aspect of life: family, work, play, and love.

A disciple of Yogananda said, "One's true spirituality is tested in the light of day." Hence, true spiritual development is revealed in one's daily life. Does one live with wisdom, compassion, vision, surrender, faith, love, peace and joy? These are the tests of a truly enlightened being.

The yogic term, *samadhi,* refers to this state of onesness or absorption into the Divine. Separation no longer exists. Each moment of life is an expression of the Divine.

It is important to note that these final states of spiritual awakening are the result of practice and letting go. It is not the ego, which is striving or "doing" that draws these divine realization, but the ability to surrender, let go and open to what is inherently our true nature.

Paramahansa Yogananda describes the various states of this ecstasy, *samadhi,* in his interpretation of the *Bhagavad Gita:*

The first stage of Divine ecstasy *(savikalpa samadhi)* gives the yogi the experience of God-union, in which no memory is present of the phenomenal universe. When he returns to mortal consciousness, he finds it hard to retain his Divine realization. By further practice of *kriya yoga,* the devotee is able to experience God-union even during the wakeful state of activities in the world. He has then achieved the "half-awake" ecstatic state, in which with open eyes he consciously sees the world around him as the Divine dream.

By development, however, the devotee is able to remain in continuous ecstasy with open or closed eyes *(nirvikalpa samadhi);* he learns to commingle his consciousness fully in the Lord and also to produce from that consciousness the dream of the cosmos. In this state he can choose to remain awake in God, without viewing the dream of creation, or he can remain in the "half-awake" blissful state, realizing the cosmos as a varied dream. When *nirvikalpa samadhi* is attained, the yogi no longer perceives the "actuality" of the world as does the ordinary man.

Modern science has discovered that the various material elements are nothing more than differently vibrating atoms. The universe is a cosmic motion picture of dancing atoms, which in turn are energy-sparks—not matter at all, but vibratory waves.[2]

The ultimate value of yogic practices and meditation is to achieve this true perception of reality and to stabilize one's consciousness within the Divine . This shift in the basic "ground of being" provides a dramatic change in one's life and one's relationships with others. All of life becomes an extension of the Divine and sacred for that reason. And while the deeper states of meditation do result in profound degrees of peace, love, and joy, the ultimate purpose is far deeper than just the attainment of these heightened states of consciousness: the *samadhi* experience transforms the individual's consciousness and nature of Being beyond the limitations of the dualistic worldly delusion.

Application for Golf:

Being in the Zone?

The "Zone" is a common term in today's world. We have the "Zone Diet" the "Zone Bar" and the "Zone" as referenced to sports. Are people talking about the same thing? Probably not, but it has become a very catchy phrase. Since we are using the term with regards to peak performance, lets take a look at what we mean by the word.

The Zone has been described with almost mystical qualities, because time changes, perceptions change of one's self and one's environment, and great results happen with what seems like little or no effort. Time seems to disappear. Visual perception changes so the cup looks bigger, greens even seem closer. Self-perception also changes. A heightened sense of self-confidence emerges, as you know you can sink that long putt. In the Zone, you feel confident and emotionally uplifted.

The Zone is a different state of awareness, and in this state, you are able to perform at your best. Individuals who have experienced being in the Zone report a sense of connection to all that is around them. There is a total integration between the mind and the body. You do not have to think about what you are doing in that state. You just will it and it happens. Your intention guides your performance. You are not in your rational mind thinking about your actions.

The Zone, as we conceive of it here, has traces of the samadhi experience. There is a sense of union, non-separation, joy, altered perception, and a heighted ability to perform. The yogic techniqes of physical postures, life force control, concentration and comtemplation open the door to this higher state. Once we have learned to shift internal consciousness and developed the capacity to maintain focus, regardless of our outer circumstances, then we play at the next level. Not everyone has the interest or discipline to achieve this goal!

Scratch golfers have told me "I just knew that the ball was going where I wanted it to go. It did not matter where the ball was. It did not matter if it was a draw or a fade. The ball was going on the green!"

Playing beyond the mind: This state of play is beyond the mind. They have reached a sense of trust and abandon in their game. This level of inner freedom opens new doors to higher levels of performance. At this level of the game, the golfer has come to trust what he or she has learned. This level of being is far beyond rational thought and perceived ideas. The zone is probably the closest experience the non-yogi will get to samadhi.

Dr. Matt Mitchell, a sport's psychologist, discussed the Zone in Golf Tips Magazine. In his article he stated, "The athlete turns off the little voices that frequently urge him or her to try a little harder, or that whisper something about the potential for failure. In the ultra-state of concentration or focus, the athlete is completely in the present. The past doesn't exist."

Modern physics and the Zone: There are some theories that might help us to understand the Zone. Modern physics and Unified Field Theory suggests that all life is part of an interconnecting flow of energy. With the help of electron microscopes, physicists have been able to observe the smallest particles in nature and discover that nothing is solid. The smallest particles became waves of energy under closer examination. As these wave patterns converge in time and space, the result is the appearance of physical, material reality. The great mystics say we hold the potential to perceive the universe as this interconnecting conscious web of energy. Modern physics and the great mystics have found common ground. Two of the best stories written about golf, *The Legend of Bagger Vance* by Steven Pressfield, and *Golf in the Kingdom* by Michael Murphy, appeal to this more mystical aspect of life.

A little help from the other side: Remember the story about my friend. Jim, who had his PGA card. He was young and relatively new on tour. His father had been a scratch golfer and really wanted him to play. Jim was a young boy in his teens when his father had died. He had avoided playing golf while his father was alive and decided to take up the game a few years after his father had died. Jim was struggling and starting to lose confidence in this tour event. In his desperation, he looked up to the sky and said, "I thought you had more pull up there." I realize what I am about to tell you may be difficult to believe. However, I swear it is the truth. I know Jim and have spent a lot of time with him. He is a man of sound character and great integrity. Jim continued to share his story. "At that moment I felt a tingling in my spine and my whole body became lighter. I felt as if something had entered me. I went on to make seven birdies in a row. My only regret is that I ran out of holes to play!"

You get my point? Who is playing golf? Who is hitting the ball? There is a lot of room inside our psyches. We can fill it up with lots of personality stuff about who we think we are, or we can learn how to get out of the way and let something greater happen. Our hidden potential is far beyond what our mind can conceive. Golf offers a great opportunity to push "the envelope of our consciousness" and discover who we really are.

Maybe there is something greater than ourselves that has a tangible influence in our lives. If you ask Jim, I think he would say so. If you ask anyone who has been touched by an angel and felt some magic in his or her life, I think he or she would say yes. If you ask anyone who has performed past their wildest imagination to greater heights than they ever dreamed possible, I think they would say yes. If you ask a parent who has prayed for the healing of their terminally ill child and seen a full spontaneous recovery, which the medical community cannot explain, I think that parent would say yes.

I have seen this magic enter peoples lives and heal them from incurable diseases, give them answers to answers to long sought questions, and fill them with hope in the midst of deep despair and worldly tragedy. Golf has long been recognized as a sport that reveals character, frustrates the intellect, and challenges the soul. It is also a game that reveals one's highest nature. The Zone is the portal to this magic kingdom.

CHAPTER 9

The Yoga Sutras of Golf
Wisdom from the Links

Our doubts are traitors,
And make us lose the good that we oft may win,
By fearing to attempt .
—William Shakespeare

The Yoga Sutras, written by the Indian sage Patanjali
are a well-known set of practical and philosophical tenets that
guide the student in the comprehensive system of spiritual
development. Estimates regarding their origin date as far back
5,000 B.C. Patanjali is credited with compiling the ideas and
practices of Raja Yoga, he was not the original creator. The
Sutras provide a guide to the practice and theoretical
understanding of yoga. Most spiritual teachers have written
interpretations of the sutras for their students. Swami
Satchidananda provides an excellent source for anyone
interested in an interpretation of Patanjali's work. Since there
are about two hundred sutras, it is well beyond the scope of
this book to discuss them in any detail. Perhaps it is sufficient

to note that they are traditionally divided into four sections: a portion on contemplation, a portion on practice, a portion on accomplishments, and finally a portion on absoluteness.

Example: In the portion on practice, Patanjali states,

"Attachment is that which follows identification with pleasurable experiences."

"Aversion is that which follows identification with painful experiences."[3]

Interpretation: If we have a positive, pleasurable experience we tend to become attached to it, we like it and want to have it around. For example, if you have a great round on a certain golf course, you really like that course and feel good when you can play there. Often times we have special holes on a course we really like because we have had a good experience there. This can even apply to people. Certain people create positive attachements. Suffering can come when we lose the object of desire and no longer have access to it. We forget that our happiness originates from within.

Conversely, if we have a bad experience, we tend to want to stay away from it. Many people have a particular hole on the course that mentally gives them trouble. They just don't think that can hit a good shot on that hole because of some mental attitude about that particular hole. It is funny how powerful the mind can be.

Personal example: I was playing golf with a couple of guys from my home course on several occassions. They were both good men, one a psychologist and the other an actor. They tended to shoot in the 80-90's and did not take the game too seriously. When I played with them, my game tended to go south as I got into their sytle and approach to the game. One day I was playing alone and having a very nice time, hitting the ball well. I happened to pass them on the fairway and hitting a practice ball, shanked it badly. They laughed and yelled out, "We really bring out the worst in your game." I begain to think, "Yes, that is true, I can't stand to play with those guys." I specifically slowed down my play so I would not catch up with them on the next hole. After they were out of sight, I went to the tee: a par three about 175 yards.

My mind was racing. I was thinking about those guys and nothing else. I knew enough to realize that I had to stop the craziness in my mind. I let it go, got focused back in the present and decided just to make a good swing. I hit a five iron square, one bounce and it was in the hole. A hole in one!

Remember, I was alone. I looked around to see if anyone saw it. If a tree falls in the forrest and there is no one around to hear it, does it make a sound? If no one saw it, it does not officially count as a hole-in-one. I did not see anyone looking my way. I went to the green and picked up the ball out of the cup. Still no one yelling for me.

I now went to the next tee. Jimmy, the actor, and his buddy were on the fairway waiving me up. I hit a good drive close to where they were standing. When I arrived I asked them if they had seen my shot. They pointed to my ball and said, "Sure, it is right there."

I said, "No, that that one, my last shot of the par three. I got a hole-in-one!"

Jimmy said, "Sure, I saw it, I just thought you chipped it in from the fairway so I didn't think much of it. I saw it, I will sign your card." I was delighted.

Five minutes ago I did not want to see this guy or play golf with him. Now I love the guy. Attachment, aversion, pleasure: I watched my mind react to all of this with its' fickle attachments. I am actually a little embarrassed to share this story, but I think it helps to make the point here.

Inspiration for the Golf Sutras: One of the great gifts of hanging around the pro- shop is being able to hear stories from the staff. It was late in the day and the flow of foot traffic had slowed into the pro shop at MountainGate Country Club. I began to talk with Patrick Boyd, a staff member and former

PGA Tour player. Patrick holds multiple course records throughout his career and spent time, on several occasions, working with sports psychologist Bob Rotella, Ph.D. Since I have a sincere interest in this area, I got Patrick talking about his time and training with Dr. Rotella. After thirty minutes of stories, Patrick pulled out a small piece of paper from the cabinet drawer and slid it across the counter.

He looked at me with a smile and said, "I shot 61 at the Willow Creek in the 1997 Utah State Open in Salt Lake City. It still stands as the course record."

He pointed to the paper that had a small list of thoughts regarding golf that Dr. Rotella had created. "I carried this with me. I just kept looking at it and reading whatever caught my attention."

Below is my list that might help you along the links. They represent much of what I have learned from helping others over the last thirty-five years.

Golf Sutras: I offer here my version of the Sutras for Golf. There are a number of practical and philosophical factors that can improve one's game.

Sutras:

- Great golf happens after lots of practice and patience. You cannot force a great round of golf.

- Your character is revealed in how you handle adversity. It is how you deal with the difficult shots, bad lies and bounces that tests the depth of your being.

- Play within your limits. Don't try to be someone you are not.

- Trust yourself. You can only be yourself, so why not give yourself a chance to play.

- Don't try so hard. A great swing is the result of rhythm, timing, and tempo. Remain relaxed and fluid and you will play better.

- You have to love to practice if you want to get good.

◆ Don't expect to make shots that you have not practiced. Miracles do happen but probably not in the rough 250 yards from the green.

◆ You will see your life reflected in your game. Just pay attention to how you approach the game and you will see the patterns of your life.

◆ Be patient. Dedication and perseverance ultimately yield great success.

◆ The breath is the link between mind and energy. Use your breath to stay focused, relaxed and in the moment.

◆ A great round of golf is wonderful, but it is not the most important thing in life. The love you share in your life is more important than a low handicap.

◆ Great putting is the simple result of rolling the ball. Find your stroke that allows you to put a good roll on the ball and then send it in the right direction.

◆ Great golfers work on their game. Practice is as important as playing.

- What you visualize will most likely come into manifestation. Use your imagination to see each shot before you hit it. Hold that image in your mind before you hit each shot.

- The power of the spoken word is profound. Be conscious of what you say about yourself and your game.

- Thoughts are real and have impact on your life and game. Develop a positive inner life and let go of the negative mind chatter.

- If you have a bad hole, don't let it get you down. A birdie can neutralize the score and get you back into the hunt.

- Be target oriented. Stay focused on a particular spot and use that as your point of reference. Swing through to the target, don't hit at the ball.

- Develop a consistent pre-game routine. Visualize your shot and create a mental plan before hitting the ball.

- The Zone is a place that will come to you. Learn to let go and be receptive to the Zone. Thinking, effort, and mechanics will not get you there.

- There is no "perfect" swing. Accept and develop what you can do to get the club square to the ball at impact.

- When you lose your swing, relax and refocus into the center of your self. Don't buy new clubs. Reconnect with the place in you that remembers how to swing.

- Learn to develop greater awareness of your body. Feel what your body is doing. Greater awareness will allow you to self-correct and maintain the harmony of good tempo and timing.

- Stay in the present moment. Thinking about your score, past or future shots will take you out of the Zone.

- Golf is a game. It is best played when you are having fun.

- There are more important things in life than winning.

- It is important to remember that a great state of mind will not overcome improper or poor technique. However, a great mental state will help you manage your game when you are not playing at your best.

- Character and integrity set the foundation for a great golfer.

- The ability for great success may require the ability to redefine who you think you are.

- Change does not come easily.

- Learning to be mentally still is more about letting go than about "doing."

- Expectations usually impair your ability to accept life.

- A great round is usually the result of successfully overcoming breakdown, not the result of perfection.

- The water in front of the green is only there if you see it.

- Discipline is the doorway to joy

CHAPTER 10

Revisiting the Ten Keys to the Zone
A gem cannot be polished without friction, nor a man
perfected without trials.
--Chinese Proverb

It is always helpful to review what we are learning. This chapter specifically focuses upon ten key factors that will enhance your ability to manage your inner life, move past your mind, and improve your chances to play in the zone.

1. PRESENCE

Stay in the moment: You must stay in the moment. Learn to bring your attention to each swing and each shot. Do not let your mind wander off into the future thinking about your score or future holes, and do not let your mind be stuck in the past on previous shots and holes.

The ability to play well requires focused attention and all of your energy and attention at the task at hand. The golf swing is very sensitive to a wandering mind. Any mental activity that is focused away from the moment will interfere with your ability to play your best.

Each time you hit the ball make it the most important thing you do and the only thing on which you are focusing. Put all of your mental energy on each shot. Think only of that shot and of nothing else. Don't think about your score and the entire game. Just stay focused on that shot, shot after shot, after shot. Stay in the moment and remain fully focused as you hit each ball. Let each shot be the beginning of your game. Forget the past, it's over. Bring a positive, fresh mental outlook to each shot.

Process Orientation: The main idea here is to stay process oriented. Anytime we start thinking about our score we tend to become outcome oriented. Once we are thinking about outcome, we are in the future. The best shots in real life are made in the moment. Our fantasy life is good for imagining shots, but if we really want to hit them great, we need to stay very focused in the present.

Breath: One powerful technique to keep yourself in the moment is to focus on your breath. Breathe from your diaphragm and feel the air come into your body. Your diaphragm is located directly under your rib cage. Place one hand on the belly and the other hand on your chest. As you inhale, allow your stomach muscles to expand and make room for the air to enter your body. It might help to imagine a balloon. The balloon expands as air enters and contracts as the air is expelled. As you breathe, your chest should not move. You want your belly to expand and contract with each breath.

Other techniques that are helpful include focusing on each step as you walk, or having your own personal mantra such as "I love golf", or "it's a wonderful day". The main goal is to avoid intense thinking.

Be a player: Take a moment to reflect on your game. I suspect you can recall a time when you were playing very well. All of a sudden you realized what you were doing. You may have started to think about your score and project what your final score might be. You might have thought about telling someone about your score. You might have begun to feel some anxiety because you were in new territory and out of your comfort zone. Any of these thoughts probably affected your score. If you are like me, pars and birdies quickly turned to bogies once the mind kicked in. One of my favorite sayings is, "You can't be a spectator and a player at the same time!" Once you are in your mind thinking about your game, you are not playing.

One shot at a time: Living in the moment can actually be a difficult thing to learn. We are accustomed to thinking about the past and planning for the future. A key to playing golf in the moment is to take each shot, one at a time. Make a plan, get committed, concentrate, feel the swing and let it go. Once you have hit the ball, be aware of what happened and learn from that shot. Now, move on to the next shot.

Develop your will: In order to successfully accomplish this task, one must have control over one's mind. Without a strong will, it is easy to let the mind and the emotions take us for a ride. Every time we react, we lose some degree of inner control or mastery, and temporarily move out of the moment. We are now back into our minds or emotions on either the roller coaster of elation or despair. You can strengthen your will by selecting a goal and completing it. Do not let anything keep you from accomplishing the goal. Now, select a more challenging goal and complete it. Each time you complete your goal and overcome any obstacles, you will be strengthening your will.

Keep your life in order: The importance of "presence" therefore requires you to have your life in order, or have a great ability to let go of mental or emotional distractions that preoccupy your attention. For example, if you have relationship problems, financial problems, emotional concerns regarding your health or the welfare of others, you might be distracted. Great golf requires a yogic attitude of gentle acceptance and detachment in order to bring all of your energy into the present moment.

Develop detachment: One final technique that is very helpful is to learn to have a detached view of what the mind creates. It is impossible to stop the various thoughts of the mind. The ones that create the most trouble on the course are the ones that say, "don't hit it in the water, don't hit it in the bunker, I can't hit this side hill lie", etc. All these negative thoughts are distractions. The trick is not to identify with them and keep your focus in the moment on something positive. A movie is a series of frames that keep moving along. You can relate to your thoughts in the same way. When a thought comes up that undermines your confidence or is a negative thought, simply be aware that it is there and then breathe and let is pass by. Do not get stuck on the thought. Just let it pass by with the breath and come back into the present. The key is not to identify with the thoughts nor take them too seriously.

2. BREATHE CORRECTLY.

Diaphragmatic Breathing: In order to relax, you need to learn to breathe right. Shallow, upper chest breathing, is not the right way to relax. Start your breath from your abdomen and use your diaphragm, then fill up your chest. As you inhale, your stomach should come out just a little bit. Studies have been done on diaphragmatic breathing. A friend of mine, Dr. Richard Miller, wrote a paper on the psychophysiology of respiration. He reviewed hundreds of studies on breathing and found that if you breathe from your diaphragm the following physical effects will result: decreased heart rate, decreased cardiopulmonary stress, decreased muscle tension, decreased fatigue, decreased need for sleep, decreased perception of pain, increased blood and oxygen to the brain and heart, alpha brain wave activation, and increased relaxation response. Proper breathing is very important. Diaphragmatic breathing is a fundamental practice in all traditions that work with energy and consciousness. Remember to practice this type of breathing and do it all the time, not just when you are playing golf.

On course breathing technique: Remember to use the special breathing technique that involves the breath and a visualization in the spine. This "pranayam" technique involves the control of life force energy. This technique will activate more right brain activity which is associated with greater visual ability and kinesthetic feel. It will speed up your ability to disengage from the mental activity of the mind and an overly mechanical approach to your swing.

3. TARGET

Target focus: Pick a specific target for each shot, whether it is your Tee-shot, a fairway shot or a putt. A common mistake is for the average golfer to just look in the general direction of where they want the ball to go. You will have greater success if you get very specific and selective for each shot. Aim towards a spot on the fairway off the tee. It might be a spot on the fairway, or another ball. It is not as effective to just think "left center"; look at the spot where you want your ball to end up.

Having a target in mind does a couple of things to help your swing. First of all, you are less likely to be hitting at the ball like you are chopping wood or hacking at weeds. If you swing towards a target you will have a better stoke and the ball will be in the way of the club as it moves towards the target. Your follow-through will be more extended and fluid if you are target oriented.

Visualize: Secondly, if you include the target into your visualization, you extend your sense of sense to encompass the goal: getting the ball into the cup. The zone has that feeling that you are connected and embracing everything around you. The cup seems bigger and closer. You can invite this experience into your awareness by expanding your sense of self to include more than just the ball lying down at your feet.

Use the will: Thirdly, maintaining a target focus also enhances your use of the "will" to put the ball in the right direction. Yogic principles teach us that energy follows thought. The will is strengthened by focused concentration and an increased flow of energy. Your dynamic will power will give you surprising results when you can maintain an internal focus on the target. Visualization helps with this process because you have to imagine that you are connected to the target.

4. TEMPO, TIMING, RHYTHM

Focus on feeling: A key to great golf during a round is to keep your focus upon the feeling aspect of your swing. If you become too mechanical and begin thinking about your swing, you are more likely to lose your fluidity and become stiff and rigid as you "try" to do the right swing. Thinking about your swing is good on the range when you are making swing changes and developing new "swing patterns" and new muscle memory.

Go with the flow: However, when you are playing on the course you have to go with what you have that day. "Trying to do something" is a certain recipe for disaster. If you are drawing the ball, then that is your game. If you are fading, so be it.

Timing: The feeling aspect of the game is your best chance for success and fun. Your sense of timing, tempo, rhythm is the feeling you have when you swing. Right timing allows for all parts of your body to work together: both the upper and lower body. Good timing will help you get the club back to a square position and maker better contact.

Don't try to kill the ball: Most average golfers try to hit the ball as hard as they can. Distance and power seem to be a big thing with the average golfer, especially men. The macho ego wants to hit it a long way, even at the expense of direction and score. I was recently playing golf with my brother who hit a Tee shot solid and straight into the woods on the left. He pulled his driver about forty yards. He comment was "I really hit that ball great!" True, but the rest of the story was in the woods and ultimate double bogey. It is good to be positive, but if you want to score well you need to play within yourself and make a swing that is in harmony with your body and is timed well. The paradox of golf is that you will ultimately hit the ball farther as you focus upon your timing and tempo because you will make more solid contact and have your weight moving more from your right side to the left. Ernie Ells is such a good example because he has such an "easy" swing, yet hits his drives well over 300 yards consistently.

Too much effort just gets in the way. Tension, especially in your hands, can cause a lot of problems. Loss of distance, shanking the ball, poor contact, and muscle strain are common results of trying too hard. You will also get more tired if you are overly tense and mentally wound up. Tension is the result of worrying, lack of trust and performance anxiety. If you let go, let the shot happen, and don't "try," paradoxically you will hit a better shot. Golf is a strange game in that "less is more."

Rhythm and timing have more to do with great shots than strength. As you are more relaxed and more flexibility, you will create greater rotation and greater club head speed, which results in more power. Remember, don't try to hit the longest shot and overpower the ball. Learn to relax and you will make better contact with the ball. The fact is, you are better off hitting the ball straight and keeping it in play, rather than trying to hit the cover off the ball and losing it out-of-bounds in the woods.

Optimum arousal: It is important to add that relaxation is not a passive, low energy condition. Focused relaxation involves bringing the will to the moment with great attention and concentration. The body is relaxed without tension, but the mind or self is fully alert, attentive and focused.

I love to watch people like Freddie Couples hit the ball because he is a master of this principle. He has such good timing and rhythm that his swing appears to be very graceful. He does not look like he is trying to hit the ball a mile, but he is very long off the tee. Great golf coaches like Butch Harmon, personal coach of Tiger Woods and Freddie Couples, advise golfers to work on the rhythm and timing if they want to gain more distance.

5. PROCESS

Being vs. doing: Great golf is a process; it is a way of being rather than doing. Total outcome focus is about "doing," rather than "being." Process allows for growth, learning and development. If you want to be perfect, you probably picked the wrong game! How you manage your game, how you recover from difficult lies, bad shots and poor breaks reveals your deeper character. Four and half hours (the average time to play 18 holes of golf) is a long time. You have a lot of time to see yourself and experience how you deal with adversity.

Self-managment: A great score is usually the result of great course management and an ability to recover from breakdown. One bad swing will often ruin an entire round for the average golfer. The person of wisdom does not over react to adversity on or off the course. He or she flows with the unfolding process, recovers quickly, learns from mistakes and stays with each moment.

This year Davis Love III won the MCI Heritage in a playoff against Woody Austin. Love won on the fourth play off hole. I was shocked that CBS showed a scene from last year's event. Woody Austin missed a 25 foot put by leaving it about twelve feet short. He took is putter and hit himself in the head about six times and so severely bent the shaft that he had to complete with round putting with his wedge. The level of frustration, rage and self-loathing that was depicted in that scene was frightening and quite disturbing. Needless to say, when the playoff came, my money was on Davis Love III. I give credit to Mr. Austin for making it into the finals and appearing to have mastered some of the demons that were unleashed during that last year's round. He is to be commended for his excellent play. However, you could still see the tension and angst in his face. He was obviously managing a lot of inner issues along with his swing.

6. PATIENCE

Never give up: Golf is a process and does tend to mirror life over a complete round. It is amazing how much can happen in four and a half hours. We can be in heaven, descend into hell, find redemption and return to grace. What a day! We can start with a bogie or worse and still have a wonderful round. There is so much golf to be played in a day that we just don't know how it will ultimately turn out. Unless we give up!! Then we know we don't have any change at all.

Patience keeps us in the game until the last stroke and keeps us coming back week after week, year after year, with the hope of improving and finding our perfect swing, even if it is just once in a round. The sound of the club striking the ball and the feel of that clean, crisp compression, rings through every cell of our body and provides a moment of wholeness and grace. Patience allows our greatness to unfold and allows us the opportunity to overcome breakdown, adversity, even failure. Patience allows us access to peace of mind, hope and faith in our deeper capacity to play at our highest level.

Trust: The yogic approach to life teaches us to be patient, to trust that there is some unfolding plan and we must play our part in the cosmic drama. We must play our part well and then wait to see how it unfolds. In *The Legend of Bagger Vance*, a book and movie that used the *Bhagavad Gita* (sacred Indian text) as the core philosophy, Bagger Vance gave Rannolf Junah sage golf advice. "It is a game that cannot be won, only played."

Stay positive: Patience also helps you to stay positive in the midst of breakdown. The worst trait of the average golfer is to become self-loathing and verbally self-abusive. Your thoughts and inner mental dialogue affect your body. The entire medical field of psychoneuroimmunology studies the relationship between the mind and the body. What you think can keep your body healthy or make you emotionally ill.

Positive thoughts create more endorphins, those chemicals released in the brain that make you feel good. I cannot tell you how many times I have heard someone on the golf course berate himself or herself after making a poor shot. Things like, "I'm stupid," "I'm a dummy," "I'm a jerk", or a lot worse, will keep you out of the Zone. Don't insult yourself or say negative things about yourself. If you really have to release some pent up frustration or negative energy, try something like "That was a really bad shot", and then forget about it. Please, do yourself a favor. Don't say "I'm a jerk" because you missed that shot! Develop a positive, forgiving, optimistic state of mind.

Stay positive and flow with each shot. You will have more fun and increase your chances of finding and staying within the Zone. Stay patient, stay in the game, and wait for things to turn around. Never give up! I have seen great golfers give up after a bad shot and mentally pull themselves out of a match. One bad hole means nothing. A birdie will bring you back into the match.

7. VISUALIZATION

Yogic philosophy suggests that energy follows thought and our consciousness is an actual field of energy. Modern quantum physics speaks to this reality as well. At the essential level, every thing is a field of interconnecting vibration. It is actually the proximity of time and space that gives these vibrations the appearance of physical, material reality. We are not isolated, nor disconnected from our environment. Our thoughts do make a difference. The love we give to others helps them in many ways. Medical research has scientifically proven that positive thoughts directed at individuals do heal others. Therefore, what we imagine can help create our reality.

When you visualize something in your mind's eye, you actually send electrical messages along neural pathways. You are programming your body and aligning your actions through this important visual preparation. Through the power of your mind, you are creating neural grooves, which lay down the patterns for your swing. Your body is responsive to your mind's images. Prepare yourself for each shot. Visualize how you want the ball to travel, where you want the ball to land. Visualize how you will swing and make contact with the ball. The power of your intention can help bring the desired result into manifestation. It is important to be very specific. Pick a spot on the fairway or a leaf as a target. Focus on a small target and hold that in your mind's eye.

Mancil Davis, also known as the "King of the Aces," holds the PGA title for the most hole-in-one's. He has fifty! He shared with me in conversation that he did not know how it worked, but he knew that he had some innate ability to really visualize the ball going into the hole on par 3's. He told me, "I can just see it going in the hole."

During a playing lesson, Todd Yoshitake, the head pro at Riviera Country Club, told me that the night before he shot a 62 in a Q-school qualifier, he visualized very hole and every shot he would make. He said the round was magical and unfolded just as he visualized it!

Remember, though we have two major ways of learning, visually and kinesthetically, the kinesthetic imagery and feeling sense actually activates micro muscle movements. Use your sense of feel and kinesthetic imagery to program your body before you hit the ball. Learn to kinesthetically remember when you have found a groove and are hitting the ball just right or putting great. Mentally practice your swing and imagine how it feels. Do this technique many, many times. The more you do it, the greater the results will be. Repetition will help your body remember. Rhythm and timing are a kinesthetic function. You need to feel the right pace. Your imagination can help create the feeling in your body.

Visualization activates hidden potentials within the psyche. Make it part of your pre-game routine.

8. TRUST

Ultimately, you have to totally trust your ability to hit or roll the ball. Fear, doubt, and disbelief often lead to mishits. The body is very sensitive to the mind's belief. Your body is unlikely to accomplish what the mind believes to be impossible. Lack of trust and faith in yourself leads to muscle contraction on the subtlest level, and thereby creates tension and a lack of fluidity and extension. Most poor shots are the result of tension and doubt and it starts in the mind.

I have seen many good golfers unable to win because of negative early childhood programming or guilt. The early messages we receive as children are deeply ingrained in our subconscious mind. Lack of love and support as children, leads to adults who do not believe they are capable or deserve to win. When the competition heats up, these early childhood thoughts and feelings will come out of the shadows and impact our adult behavior. Guilt will result in adult life when we lose touch with our integrity and act in ways that are hurtful to others or ourselves. Guilt will keep us from wining. It undermines are sense of worth and value and keeps us from being the best we can be.

There is an inner childhood state where freedom, trust and the joy of play is the foundation for being. If we can reconnect with our love of the game and our trust in ourselves, then more joy and freedom is possible in the game.

In the final seconds, letting go and freely hitting the ball is what brings success. Use whatever methods work for you to clear away any thoughts or feelings that keep you from trusting your innate ability to play or make you feel like you don't deserve to win.

In a land far away, a long time ago, a King had the best music stand maker in the kingdom. He had such a gift to make exquisite music stands. The people in the local village had to know his secret. They organized a committee to find the music stand maker and discover his secret. The small group of local townsmen went to the castle and found the King's music stand maker. He was living way in the back of the castle. Upon inquiry, he revealed his secret. "It is actually rather easy. I begin by fasting here in the castle for five days. I then go out into the forest and walk around for another five day, still fasting. I then walk around and around until I am totally lost, disoriented and delirious. At this point I look up and see the most exquisite music stand I have ever seen. I then simply cut away all the wood surrounding the music stand."

9. COMMIT TO EACH SHOT.

Hesitation and doubt can lead to disaster. It has been said by many great golf teachers that the wrong club swung with complete commitment is better than the right club swung with doubt. You can see this very clearly on the green. A mental commitment to the line will allow for a firm stroke and will roll the ball on line. Doubt tends to make you want to hold back, especially on a fast green, resulting in a slow pace and deceleration that often lets the ball roll off line.

Commitment relates to the entire mind-body connection. Most golfers tend to make a poor shot when they are caught in doubt about which club to hit. You can see it in the address: they don't look comfortable and the air of confidence is nowhere to be found. Commitment brings into focus the subtle alignment of mind and body. It is also very difficult to maintain target focus when the commitment is shaky.

10. NON-ATTACHMENT.

The concept of non-attachment lies at the core of yoga philosophy. The deeper challenge of selflessness is to act without attachment to the results. This balanced state leads to greater peace of mind and equanimity in action because there is less reaction to outcome, an ideal mental state for golfer. Non-attachment encourages one to act, to do his/her best and let go of the results. It takes a mature understanding of life to know that things do not always unfold as we would like, and that might be for the best. Life also seems to test us at every bend in the road. Success rarely occurs without overcoming adversity. An attitude of non-attachment allows us to stay in the game, to stay in life's process and patiently persevere to reach our goal of success.

Release expectations: Furthermore, the ability stay in the moment and let go of performance or outcome concerns is directly connected to one's level of attachments and expectations. There is a saying, "Expectations lead to suffering." This is so because we become emotionally distraught when we do not perform at the level that we have decided, "we should" perform.

Our ideas about our game create most of our distress. Our expectations, and our emotional attachment to those expectations, begin in the mind and create the seeds of distraction. Inner freedom results when we can release all expectations. Hit each ball and play it as it lies.

Great champions are defined by their ability to overcome adversity and hold up under pressure. Difficult lies, unexpected bounces, and "bad breaks" provide the stage for great comebacks. One cannot demonstrate the ability to overcome adversity if difficulty never presents itself. A change in attitude and perspective can make a huge difference in one's approach to life.

So that's it. If you practice these ten points, your golf game is going to be a lot more fun and you're going to play much better. You might be surprised to see how other areas in your life also improve.

CHAPTER 11

Resources for Learning

He who asks is a fool for five minutes, but he who does not ask remains a fool forever.
Chinese Proverb

Developing new skills is always a process. Real learning is more than an intellectual task: changes must become integrated in our cellular structure, our muscles memory, consciousness itself. To that aim, there are a variety of useful tools to help you develop the skills that we have discussed in this book. The following is a list of recommended resources:

Most are available at www.ronmann.com

Please call 866-816-1026 if you have any questions.

Zone CD Training

Find the Zone:
Master the Mental Game of Golf
by Ron Mann, Ph.D.

The Find the Zone CD is designed to give you the best learning tools possible. I have used these methods for more than twenty years. They are proven techniques that have helped people focus, relax and control inner states. Research with college golfers at UC Davis demonstrated that they tended to play more consistently and achieve lower scores when they listened to the *Find the Zone* CD. The UCLA women's golf team used these techniques during the 2001 season and came in 5th at the National Championship. They had not been able to even qualify for Nationals since 1997.

Meditation

Inspiration for Meditation

This CD was originally produced in Kauai, Hawaii. The guided meditation focuses upon the Chakra system and the life force energy in the spine. The breath and mantra are used to develop concentration and redirect the life force energy away from the outer senses into the deeper centers of the brain. The intent is upon the direct experience of the self as love, joy and light, not merely the physical, emotional or mental. Original music created and performed by Aryeh David. (60 minutes)

Zen Meditation

This meditation tape arises out of the Zen tradition. Simple bamboo flute music becomes the backdrop for mindful awareness. The focus is upon becoming aware of the contents of the mind and emotions without being identified with them. The feeling is simple and elegant. Original music created and performed by Aryeh David. (60 minutes-Music continues for extended meditation on side B.)

Om Mani Padme Hum (Chanting CD)

This ancient and sacred Tibetan chant is combined with the Classical Indian Tambura. Chanting is a profound way to shift your consciousness because the vibration in sound directly affects the nervous system. A profound sense of peace and a deepening of the meditation state is obtained when one merges the mind with the sound. The words Om (Cosmic sound of creation) Mani (Lotus) Padme (Jewel) strongly impact your consciousness. Tambura played by Brian Godden. (60 minutes-21 minutes of chanting and 19 minutes of Tambura music for meditation.)

Tension Control

Self Hypnosis for Stress Release (audio cassette)
An intensive hypnotic induction helps you to totally relax and release stress. The process focuses upon entire body relaxation and visual imagery for a safe haven in nature. The music is beautiful, the pace is slow and inviting. You will learn very useful techniques for deep relaxation. Original music created and performed by Aryeh David. (60 minutes-Music continues for extended relaxation on side B.)

The Tension Meter from GolfPsych

 This is a biofeedback instrument that measures heart rate variability. The unit consists of a strap around the chest and a small case with digital display. It is very sensitive and accurately provides immediate feedback regarding emotional and mental activity. Can be used during play and off-course for training.

Hatha Yoga

Every city has yoga studios that offer classes of all levels. The important thing is to find a class that is right for you. Avoid yoga classes that are more like calisthenics. Look for a class that integrates the breath with each posture.

Personality Development

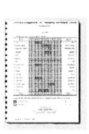 The GolfPsych Report compares your personality with Golf Professionals on Tour who have won major tournaments. It is scientifically validated and very insightful. The information helps you to fine tune your personality for competitive golf.

Golf Fitness Equipment

Flexi Club by Lee Brandon
www.leebrandoninc.com
The strength and stretching device can be used on and off the course.

Books

Pressfield Steven, *The Legend of Bagger Vance,*
    HarperCollins, 2000.

Murphy, Michael, *Golf and the Kingdom.* Penguin USA
    Reprint edition, 1997.

Payne, Larry, *Yoga RX.* New York, Broadway Books, 2002.

Mann, Ronald. *Sacred Healing: Integrating Spirituality with
    Psychotherapy.* Los Angeles, Institute of Alternative
    Healing, 2001.

Yogananda, Paramahansa, *Autobiography of a Yogi.* Los
    Angeles, Self Realization Fellowship, 1971.

Satchidananda, Swami. *Integral Yoga: The Yoga Sutras of
    Pantanjali,* Pomfret Center, Integral Yoga
    Publications, 1978.

Shoemaker, Fred & Pete. *Extraordinary Golf - The Art of the Possible*. Perigee, 1997.

Golf and the Spirit by Ram Das. Audio Cassette through the Shivas Irons Society.

Mental Coaching

Dr. Mann is available for coaching in person, through email and telephone contact. He is also assciated with the GolfPsych network and may be able to help you find a mental golf coach in your area.

He may be reached at:

Phone: 866-816-1026

Email: mannr@ronmann.com

Website: www.ronmann.com

About the Model

Yoga with *Suzanne*

therapeutic to athletic
- Group/Private Yoga
- Shiatsu Acupressure
- Gift Certificates Available

Suzanne Strachan
Cert. Yoga Instructor/Acupressurist since 1985
Member of Int'l. Assoc. of Yoga Therapists & CA. Yoga Teachers Assoc.

818-620-0132

Suzanne Strachan, CYT, CMT began practicing hatha yoga in 1981 and has been a certified yoga instructor/therapist and shiatsu acupressurist since 1985. She's also been a devotee of Parmahansa Yogananda since 1987.

Suzanne integrates shiatsu acupressure with the yoga for those students with specific needs such as back, shoulder and hip issues, as well as carpel tunnel syndrome, osteoporosis and arthritis to release energy and holding patterns. Students of hers who are sports enthusiasts, from black belt martial artists to "weekend golfers" have enjoyed improved range of motion from a tailored combination of yoga and shiatsu.

She teaches for such diverse groups as Rocketdyne Boeing employees, a group of 11-13 year old boys with ADD, seniors, yoga studios, Self Realization Fellowship women's group, parks and rec. and private students for therapy or improved performance. She is sought out by gyms like Gold's Gym and Tanny's Personal Fitness. Her past resume credits have included teaching for Pepperdine University, the Thousand Oaks Teen Center and a martial arts studio.

You may reach Suzanne at: yoga2serv@cs.com
www.yogawithsuzanne.com
818-620-0132

160

Notes

[1] Paramahansa Yogananda, *God Talks with Arjuna: The Bhagavad Gita.* Los Angeles: Self-Realization Fellowship, 1995, p. 74.

[2] Paramahansa Yogananda, *God Talks with Arjuna: The Bhagavad Gita.* Los Angeles: Self-Realization Fellowship, 1995, p. 559.

[3] Satchidananda, Swami, *Ingegral Yoga: The Yoga Sutras of Patanjali.* Connecticut: Integral Yoga Publications, 1978, p. 106.

Index

U

Unified Field Theory 117

V

Visual imagery 108
visualization 36, 92, 96, 97, 107, 108, 110, 136, 137, 138, 146, 148

W

Warm Up Routine 49
Warrior I 56
Willow 60
Woody Austin 142
www.ronmann.com 153

Y

yamas 23
Yoga 1, 4, 5, 7, 11
Yoga Sutras 121, 158
Yogic Crunch 64
Yogic philosophy 146

Z

Zone 1, 7, 8, 19, 29, 116, 117, 120, 128, 129, 131, 133, 138, 145, 154

About the Author

Ron Mann, Ph.D. is an internationally recognized author, teacher and Peak Performance Coach. As a licensed clinical psychologist, he was in private practice from 1976 through 2002. He is a certified hatha yoga instructor from Samata Yoga International and a disciple of Paramahansa Yogananda, practicing Kriya Yoga since 1979. His book, *Sacred Healing: Integrating Spirituality with Psychotherapy,* reached the L.A. Times Healthy Bestseller list in 1998. He has also produced a series of audio programs for golf and personal development. His audio CD, *Find the Zone: Master the Mental Game of Golf,* was reviewed in Golf Magazine, Links Magazine and Golf in Florida Magazine.

Dr. Mann has successfully shared his understanding of peak performance with UCLA Women's Golf Team, Lee Brandon (2001 RE/MAX World Woman's Long Drive Champion), UC Davis Men's Golf Team, PGA teaching staff at Riviera and MountainGate Country Clubs and numerous high school and amateur players. Dr. Mann has been on Fox Sports Net discussing Tiger Woods and numerous radio talk shows.

He is a member at MountainGate Country Club, holds a single digit handicap and has two hole-in-ones. He is located in the Pacific Palisades, California and is available for individuals, teams and businesses. He can be reached through his website at www.ronmann.com.